SATAN
HIS
PERSON
AND
POWER

Other Books by the Same Author

All About Bible Study
All the Men of the Bible
The Women of the Bible
All the Miracles of the Bible
All the Parables of the Bible
All the Prayers of the Bible
All the Doctrines of the Bible
All the Kings and Queens of the Bible
All the Children of the Bible
All the Promises of the Bible
All the Books and Chapters of the Bible
All the Holy Days and Holidays
All the Trades and Occupations of the Bible
All the Apostles of the Bible
All the Messianic Prophecies of the Bible
All the Divine Names and Titles of the Bible
The Funeral Sourcebook
The Lenten Sourcebook
The Man Who Changed the World (2 vols.)
The Week That Changed the World
Last Words of Saints and Sinners
The Sins of Saints
The Gospel of the Life Beyond
The Unseen Army
Twin Truths of Scripture (2 vols.)
Triple Truths of Scripture (3 vols.)
How to Find Comfort in the Bible
Seven Words of Love
The Man Who Died for Me

SATAN
HIS
PERSON
AND
POWER

HERBERT LOCKYER

WORD PUBLISHING
Dallas · London · Sydney · Singapore

SATAN: HIS PERSON AND POWER

Unless otherwise indicated, all Scripture quotations are from the King James Version.

Quotations marked RSV are from the Revised Standard Version of the Bible, copyrighted 1946, 1952, © 1971, 1973 by the Division of Christian Education of the National Council of Churches of Christ in the U.SA., and used by permission. Those marked Moffatt are from *The Bible: A New Translation* by James Moffatt, © 1922, 1924, 1926, 1935, 1950, 1952, 1953, 1954 by Harper and Brothers, Inc. and are used by permission. Passages marked Weymouth are from *Weymouth's New Testament in Modern Speech* by Richard Frances Weymouth, as revised by J. A. Robertson, by permission of Harper and Row, Inc. and James Clarke and Company Limited.
Those marked NIV are from *The Holy Bible: the New International Version,* © 1978 by the New York International Bible Society, used by permission.

ISBN: 0-8499-3218-1
Library of Congress Catalog Card Number: 80-50816

012349 RRD 987654321

Printed in the United States of America

Contents

*An understanding of satanic forces is
of the most vital importance to believers
who would learn to successfully withstand
the prince of this world.*

Introduction

While we consider the subject before us to be of the most solemn and serious nature, there may be those who think a comprehension of the personality and power of the prince of darkness is unprofitable. Far from being of little importance, such a theme is most valuable and vital. Our individual condition before God and man turns upon our understanding of what the Bible teaches us about the identity and influence of the one whom Paul described as "the god of this world." A famous general was once asked the secret of his success in war, and he replied, "I take in the power of the enemy."

It is, therefore, necessary for every believer who would wage a successful spiritual warfare against his avowed and diabolical enemy, to ascertain a knowledge of his history and might so as to victoriously withstand him. The majority of people have a vague idea that there is a kind of evil genius at work in the world, but all too few are cognizant of his power to bring humanity under his tyranny and diabolical sway. If there is no such a person as the devil, then who is responsible for the depraved state of society today? Behind evil forces there must be an evil figure responsible for them. More than fifty years ago Mr. Alfred J. Hough composed the following apt lines:

Men don't believe in a Devil now, as their fathers used to do;
They've forced the door of the broadest creed to let his majesty
          through.
There isn't a print of his cloven foot or a fiery dart from his bow
To be found on earth or in air today, for the world has voted so.

But who is it mixing the fatal draught that palsies heart and
          brain,
And loads the bier of each passing year with ten hundred
          thousand slain?
Who blights the bloom of the land today with the fiery breath of
          hell,
If the Devil isn't and never was won't somebody rise and tell?

Who dogs the steps of the toiling saint and digs the pit for his
          feet?
Who sows the tares in the field of time wherever God sows His
          wheat?
The Devil is voted not to be, and, of course the thing is true;
But who is doing the kind of work the Devil alone should do?

We are told that he doesn't go about as a roaring lion now;
But whom shall we hold responsible for the everlasting row
To be heard in church, in home, and state, to earth's remotest
          bounds;
If the Devil by a unanimous vote is nowhere to be found?

Won't somebody step to the front forthwith, and make their
          bow, and show
How the frauds and crimes of a single day spring up? We want to
          know.
The Devil was fairly voted out, and, of course, the Devil's gone;
But simple people would like to know who carries his business
          on!

Spiritual minds are convinced that we live in days of advanced satanism when, knowing that he has but a short time left on earth, Satan is showing great wrath. As the god of this world he is flooding his domain with putrid pleasures and pursuits. His coteries must not be given time to think of any peril involved in obeying their god. So we have the casting off of any restraint. Gone are the days when reserve held sway. Violence, corruption, vandalism, and laxity in sex relationships that would have shocked our grandparents a century or so ago are now a common part of modern life. We live in an age of unwholesome and widely publicized suggestiveness. The world is given over to sin. *Rotten* is a mild term to depict the moral condition of our much vaunted civilization.

Is it not, therefore, imperative for the Christian to understand the devices of the enemy of mankind responsible for this universal corruption and crime? The only authoritative and accurate knowledge he can gather regarding the adversary's activities is found in the Scriptures and these the devil would love to destroy. From first to last, the Bible is a Book of battles. Satan engages in a deadly conflict with both God and man, and both man and God are found arrayed against their mutual archenemy. Then God is found striving against man, and man is seen defying God; and man is seen at war with man.

But it is the devil who comes before us as the bitterest foe of heaven and earth. No matter where you turn you find this created, personal, evil one presented as the adversary of God and man, of Christ and of the Christian, of holiness and truth. What a startling record the Bible gives of his unceasing antagonism toward heavenly and human forces! How pressing is our need to study with Spirit-anointed eyes the wiles and stratagems of Satan to overthrow the eternal counsels and purposes of God, and then to behold how gloriously he is defeated at every point by One who is "greater than he"!

In conclusion, it may be fitting to utter a word of warning regarding any levity when speaking of the devil and his works. No one with any conception of how dangerous Satan is, both to ourselves and to the holy cause we represent, can ever speak of him in a jocular way, or engage in flippant language regarding his personality or his work. All unwarranted appellations, such as *Old Nick*, are to be deprecated. When Michael the Archangel came into conflict with Satan, remembering his previous glory and dignity, he did not judge him over the matter of the body of Moses, but left him to the Lord. He said, "The Lord rebuke thee" (Jude 9). See also Zechariah 3:1,2.

HIS PERSON
&POWER

1

Satan in Profile

It is somewhat amazing that although there are abundant references in Scripture to the origin and operations of Satan, some theologians fail to find him therein, even though our Lord mentions him some fifteen times, under different names, all of which prove his actuality and personality.

Dr. Ramsey, when Archbishop of Canterbury, conducted a question and answer session among Cambridge undergraduates, and when asked a question about the reality of Satan replied: "I do not draw from the Bible the inference that there is an individual monarch of evil. I think it is too dogmatic to say that evil spirits have had the best of it."

One wonders what kind of Bible the genial Archbishop reads. It must be one from which all references to a personal devil and hosts of evil spirits have been omitted. Evidently this notable church leader does not accept the revelation of John that "the whole world lieth in wickedness" or as the RSV expresses it, "the whole world is in the power of the evil one" (1 John 5:19).

1. His Origin

The question has been asked, "Where did the devil come from?" The answer is that he had a magnificent beginning, for he came from God, the Creator of all, even of all angelic beings. We must hasten to add that he was not created a *devil*, but became one through his own volition. He came from God as *Lucifer*, the highest of the order of the Seraphim, and was anointed for a position of great authority. All things that are in heaven and in earth visible and invisible were created by Christ and for him, probably, before the creation of material things, in the garden of God—a primeval place of God's original Eden rather than the one of Genesis 3. (See Col. 1:16; Ezek. 28:11–19.)

Scripture states that Satan was *created* as a *cherub*, and *full of wisdom and perfect in beauty* (Ezek. 28:12,14,15). But although he was the highest being among the angelic creatures created by God, what an immeasurable gulf exists between the uncreated, self-existent eternal Person of the Godhead and Lucifer, the chief of God's creatures. The two great portions of Scripture containing valuable information regarding the early history of Satan are Isaiah 14:12–14 and Ezekiel 28:11–19. These passages should be prayerfully studied by all searchers for truth, seeing they go beyond the earthly persons mentioned and point to a supernatural being of some kind.

2. His Fall

At his creation, he was given the name *Lucifer*, meaning Day-Star, The Light-bearer, Son of the morning, and was set upon the holy mountain of God. For awhile, he was perfect in his ways (Isa. 14:12; Ezek. 28:15). But through his own folly *Lucifer* became *The Prince of Darkness*. Yet now, in his evil seductiveness, he can transform himself into an angel of light to deceive the souls of men.

What was it that caused this exalted being to fall from his high and privileged position? In his preexistent state, Jesus witnessed Satan falling as lightning from heaven, and Isaiah describes him as being "brought down" (see Isa. 14:12,15; Luke 10:18). Peter speaks of him being cast down to hell with all the other rebellious angels (2 Peter 2:4). Jude says they failed to keep their first estate, but left their own habitation, or as the *New International Version* puts it, "The angels . . . did not keep their positions of authority but abandoned their own home" (Jude 6). Cast out of heaven into the air, the latter sphere has since been the scene and center of Satan's power as "the prince of the power of the air" (Eph. 2:2).

Sin did not commence when Eve took the forbidden fruit in Eden, but in a past eternity when, as *Lucifer*, lifted up with pride, he challenged God (1 Tim. 3:6). Being perfect in beauty made him proud, and his brightness brought about his corruption. Before his fall, he covered God's throne or guarded it. But, not satisfied with covering it, he *coveted* it, and so fell. He wanted to be, not an emissary of God, but equal with God, or even *above* God. How expressive are his five *I will's* as given by Isaiah:

I will ascend into heaven,
I will exalt my throne *above* the stars of God:
I will sit also upon the mount of the congregation . . .:
I will ascend above the heights of the clouds:
I will be like the most High (Isa. 14:13,14).

But when God discovered iniquity in the one he created perfect in his ways, he described Satan's doom for his covetousness in six *I will's* of his own:

I will cast thee as profane out of the mountain of God: . . .
I will destroy thee, O covering cherub. . . .
I will cast thee to the ground,
I will lay thee before kings. . . .

I [will] bring forth fire from the midst of thee, it shall
devour thee . . .
I will bring thee to ashes upon the earth (Ezek. 28:16–18).

Solomon reminds us that "Pride goeth before destruction, and an haughty spirit before a fall" (Prov. 16:18), and
this certainly depicts the reason for Satan's expulsion from
heaven. The middle letter of *pride* is *I*, just as it is in sin,
and it was the big *I* that brought about the fall of Lucifer.
This is how he became the devil. Pride caused him to
"opposeth and exalteth himself above all that is called
God, or that is worshipped; so that he as God sitteth in the
temple of God, shewing himself that he is God," deceiving
many by his "power" and "lying wonders." This "son of
perdition" will be the ape of the devil (2 Thess. 2:3–11).

With all his created gifts, Lucifer failed to recognize that
the Creator is always greater than the creature he had
made. He did not sense the essential difference between
himself and his Creator who, in effect, rebuked him in the
words, "Thou thoughtest that I was altogether such an one
as thyself" (Ps. 50:21). The only one "equal with God" is
his beloved Son (John 5:18). Lucifer, then, became the
devil when he failed to see his proud rebellion against God
as sin. Since then, however, he knows only too well into
what pit and from what height he has fallen, and the
tragedy of his eternal loss.

3. His Aliases

As a noun, *alias* implies an assumed name, and Scripture provides us with a long list of the aliases of him who is
the adversary of both God and man. Often in Scripture a
name is indicative of the holder's character and conduct.
For instance, *Nabal* means "a fool," so we have the plea of
Abigail, his wife, before David, "Let not my lord, I pray
thee, regard this man of Belial, even Nabal: for as his name
is, so is he" (1 Sam. 25:25).

It is so with the manifold designation of Satan, "As his names, so is he." Taken together they describe his corrupt heart and evil work. Among the principal names he goes by, we have, first of all—

Satan

Occurring some fifty times in Scripture, this designation means an adversary or opposing spirit. It is derived from *shatana* and implies "to be adverse," "to hate," "to accuse." The first mention of him in this capacity is in connection with David, "He *[Satan]* moved David to number Israel" (2 Sam. 24:1; 1 Chron. 21:1). If we allow ourselves to be "moved" by Satan, the action he prompts us to do will be in the nature of it, adverse to the will of God, as in the form of hatred for his purpose. In Job 1:6, the margin gives us *adversary* for "Satan."

Devil

In the Old Testament we have frequent references to "devils," meaning evil, seducing demons, but Satan as *the* devil is not so named. But in the New Testament he is described thus almost forty times. In some cases the term *devil* implies a demon or fallen angelic being (as in the malady of one who was "possessed with a devil," or a demon as the RSV indicates). But when the verse revolves around the prince of devils or demons, he is always described as *the* devil. "That old serpent, called the Devil" (Rev. 12:9; 20:10). Both names are combined in Peter's warning, "your *adversary* the *devil*" (1 Peter 5:8; Rev. 12:9). The derivation of the name is meaningful, for *devil* is from *diabolus, dia,* implying "down," and *ball,* "to throw down." It was in this form he appeared to Jesus in the effort to tempt him to act adversely to clear teaching of Scripture. He said, "Cast thyself down" (Matt. 4:6). The devil has the power to throw one down (Luke 9:42), but with Jesus his effort was unavailing. Cast down, and cast out of heaven at the time of his revolt, the devil is unceasing in his diabolical work of throwing humans down.

Serpent

Paul saw in the serpent who beguiled Eve the subtlety of Satan (2 Cor. 11:3; Gen. 3:1,13. See Rev. 12:9,14,15; 20:2). References to serpents can be used to illustrate the subtle, dangerous work of that "old serpent, the devil." The first promise of redemption appears in Genesis 3:15 when God said to Satan, "I will put enmity between thee and the woman, and between thy seed and her seed; it shall bruise thy *head*, and thou shalt bruise his heel." The serpent's chief care of itself is for its head, because its heart is under its throat. By his death, Jesus, who came as the seed of the woman, bruised the *head* of "the old serpent." When he cried, "It is finished," he manifested his power as the Conquering One in his destruction of the works of the devil. Jesus robbed Satan of his power and authority.

Among other titles for Satan, we have that of—

Prince

"Prince of this world" (John 12:31).
"Prince of demons" (Matt. 9:34, RSV).
"Prince of the power of the air" (Eph 2:2).

God of this world (2 Cor. 4:4).
Angel of Light (2 Cor. 11:14).
Liar and the father of lies (John 8:44, RSV).
Beelzebub (Matt. 10:25; 12:24).
Belial (2 Cor. 6:15).
Dragon (Rev. 12:9).
Abaddon—Apollyon, both of which mean "destroyer" (Rev. 9:11).

Adversary (1 Peter 5:8).
Roaring Lion (1 Peter 5:8).
Murderer (John 8:44).
Evil one (Matt. 6:13, RSV).
Tempter (Matt. 4:3).
Accuser (Rev. 12:10).
Thief (John 10:10).

What a revelation these striking designations provide of the diabolical power of such a fiend! Yet Dr. Ramsey, the one-time ecclesiastical head of the Anglican Church, cannot find evidence of a monarch of evil in the Bible! It is incumbent upon us to know the nature, character, tactics of our enemy, for only then can we resist him. And the promise is, "Resist the devil, and he will flee from you" (James 4:7). Submitting ourselves to the Lord, and trusting in him, we are more than conquerors over the wiles of the devil.

4. HIS POWER

While the titles we have considered emphasize the power of the devil, it is necessary to examine what such power entails. Although, when he sinned against God he lost his exalted position as *Lucifer,* is now a fallen, degraded being, and was judged by the cross (John 12:31; 16:11; Col. 2:15), he has lost but little of his power. Christ did not deny Satan's declaration that he had power over the kingdoms of this world, which kingdoms he said were delivered unto him, and which power he can bestow on whom he will (Luke 4:6). We are told that he likewise had the power of death, but that this power was surrendered to Christ when by dying, he defeated death (Heb. 2:14; Rev. 1:18).

Job records that Satan had power over sickness, and physical infirmities are attributed to him in the Gospels

(Job 2:1–8; Luke 13:16). He was able to sift Peter as wheat in a sieve (Luke 22:31). Evil ones were delivered unto him for judgment (1 Cor. 5:5). Satan is also said to have weakened the nations, to have made the earth to tremble, to shake kingdoms, to have made the earth a wilderness, destroying the cities, and not to have opened the house of his prisoners (Isa. 14:12–17). Jude said that Michael the archangel dared not contend against his power (v. 9). Throughout the world today Satan is behind the scenes in international and national policies and problems; he is the instigator of the corrupt and violent condition of human society.

Yes, Satan has widespread power but he is not omnipotent, nor does he possess power beyond limit. Jesus could say, "*All* power is given unto me in heaven and earth," an assertion to which Satan cannot lay claim. Under grace his power is controlled and the believer can experience victory over him through the blood of the Lamb and the power of the Spirit (Eph. 2:2–11; 6:10–12; 1 John 4:4; Rev. 12:11). The demons Jesus cast out of the man who had lived in the tombs begged him to influence a herd of swine to receive them—a tribute to his superior power. The swine, however, preferred suicide by drowning rather than demon-possession (Matt. 8:32). Jesus is able to deliver souls from Satan's bondage (Luke 13:16). Satan's power to inflict physical impediment and infirmity and pain can be overruled for the believer's spiritual enrichment (2 Cor. 12:7–10).

Fallen, then, from his high estate, Satan retains certain qualities. He can take captive—"devour," "put to sleep" (Matt. 25:5; 26:40–41; 2 Tim. 2:26; 1 Peter 5:8). But although he has great wisdom and power, he is not omniscient as his Creator is. Without doubt, he is a close and continual observer of the movements of God and the ways of men, but he lacks the foreknowledge, insight, and perception of deity. Neither is he omnipresent, meaning he does not have the ability to be everywhere at the same time, which is the prerogative of the Godhead alone. Yet, as we shall see, he has legions of fallen angels under his control. These move to and fro throughout the earth, and with these he is in constant touch. Jesus could have had twelve legions of unfallen angels to help him if aid were needed (Matt. 26:53). Demons are so numerous that through them Satan is practically everywhere (see Eph. 6:12, RSV).

5. His Work

Christ died to destroy the works of the devil. They are manifold and disastrous, with his strategies and warfare directed against the Trinity, Scripture, and the saints of God. Nothing is said about his warfare against the unregenerate for they are his own, and therefore under his authority and control (John 8:44; 1 John 5:19, RSV). Scripture portrays his character as being presumptuous, proud, mighty, wicked, malignant, subtle, deceitful, fierce, and cruel. His conduct displays the same traits, as the following outline proves—

He tempts (Matt. 4:3–10).
He perverts Scripture (Ps. 91:11,12; Matt. 4:5,6).
He opposes God's works (Zech. 3:1; 1 Thess. 2:18).
He hinders the gospel (Matt. 13:19; 19:22; 2 Cor. 4:4).
He works lying wonders (2 Thess. 2:9; Rev. 16:14).
He assumes many disguises (2 Cor. 11:14; 1 Peter 5:8; Rev. 12:9).
He defiles good works (Matt. 13:19–30).
He blinds multitudes to the truth (2 Cor. 4:4).
He strives unceasingly to prevent faith (Luke 8:12; Acts 13:8–10).
He endeavors to damage or destroy faith (Job 1; Matt. 13:39; Luke 22:31; 1 Peter 5:8,9).
He creates doubt and denial (Gen. 3:1–5).

Satan is more an enemy of faith than of morals because morality with unbelief suits his subtle purpose. He knows that the natural, unregenerate heart of unbelief tends to wrong-doing of its own accord (Rom. 8:7; James 1:14; Mark 7:21). In his "deep things" Satan apes "the deep things of God." As an "angel of light," he seeks to outshine him who is "*the* Light of the World." For the human dupes of the devil there is the glorious hope of emancipation and transformation through all Christ accomplished by his death and resurrection, and through the regenerating power of the Holy Spirit. But for the devil himself there is no hope of change. His character and doom are fixed. In his *Paradise Lost*, Milton gives us a unique portrayal of the devil's degenerate and defiled mind. As Lucifer, he assured his chief lieutenant, Beelzebub, that in spite of all that God had done in deposing him, he would never change—

> Though changed in outward lustre; that fixt mind
> And high disdain, from sense of injured merit,
> That with the mightiest raised me to contend,
> And to the fierce contention brought along
> Innumerable forces of spirits armed
> That durst dislike His reign, and me preferring,
> His utmost power with adverse power opposed
> In dubious battle on the Plains of Heaven,
> And shook His throne.

6. His Angels

When Satan revolted, he claimed with manifest falsity no inward change in him as *Lucifer* had taken place. He insisted it was evil in God's rule and preference for his own just cause that prompted his revolt. As John Milton vividly describes above, the tragedy was that he brought a host of fellow angelic beings into the conflict with God who shared in his expulsion from heaven and likeness in the termination of divine service. When Jesus said, "I beheld Satan as lightning fall from heaven," he implied that the angels also who followed Satan in his challenge to God, fell with him (Luke 10:17,18). "The dragon fought and his angels . . . and his angels were cast out with him" (Rev. 12:7–9).

Jude refers to "the angels which kept not their first estate" (Jude 6). Peter speaks of "the angels that sinned" (2 Peter 2:4). Our Lord himself spoke of the armies of the evil one, as "the devil and his angels" (Matt. 25:41). The inference from these references is that an unnumbered army of angels fell with Satan. Many of these evil beings became identified with the false gods of the heathen. The Jews called Beelzebub "the god of Ekron" (2 Kings 1:2) and "the prince of the devils" (Matt. 12:24). By way of contrast, we have "his Father with his angels" (Matt. 16:27; Rev. 3:5). Paul warned the Corinthians of the danger of joining in heathen festivals with their "sacrifice to devils" (1 Cor. 10:20,21).

We read much in the Gospels about people possessed by "devils," or more correctly "demons" as the RSV states it. There is only *one* devil, and the one is more than enough. As the emissaries of Satan the demons never cease their activities, for in their originally created form as angels they have no need of sleep or rest. Through the ages they have a much more subtle form causing some to depart from the faith through their devilish doctrines (1 Tim. 4:1). While the term "demon" does not occur in the ASV, these evil spirits are separated into two divisions.

First, there are those who are *fettered.*

Jude, in his category of those angelic creatures who kept not their first estate, speaks of those who were immediately chained and cast into darkness as soon as they fell. Deposed, they were bound, and since then have been inoperative as wicked spirits. Because of their perpetual bondage, they are beyond the bidding of their satanic lord (2 Peter 2:4). One wonders who the angelic perverts were to whom Christ preached in their prison (1 Peter 3:19). Did he proclaim to these doomed spirits the blood-bought victory over all satanic powers he had secured for the sinning sons of men, and of the ultimate eternal judgment of the devil and all his angels?

Second, there are those who are *free.*

These subjects of Satan are, like their evil master, adversaries of both God and man, and being free, roam the earth fulfilling their lord's commands. Many of these *demons* are prominent in heathen mythology, and are referred to by the psalmist, "The gods of the heathen are demons" (Ps. 96:5, LXX). See 1 Corinthians 10:20. For a full and exhaustive study of this important phase of biblical truth the reader is referred to the author's chapter on "The Doctrine of Satan and the Demons," in his volume *All the Doctrines of the Bible,* published by Zondervan. Briefly stated these unfettered messengers of Satan are:

Personal spirits, who can walk, seek, will, find, and take (Matt. 12:43–45).

They are Satan's cohorts, his "kingdom," his "angels," his "Legion" (Matt. 12:26,27; 25:41; Mark 5:9).

They seek embodiment in man or beast and control all they enter (Matt. 12:43,44; Mark 5:12).

Their characteristics are given as "exceeding fierce," "violent," "unclean" (Matt. 8:28,32; 10:1).

Their works are manifold and disastrous.

Demons can stimulate physical maladies in those they possess. We distinguish between real mental disease and *mental disorder* produced by demon possession. Demons can cause "dumbness" (Matt. 9:33), "epilepsy" (Matt. 17:14–18, RSV), paralysis (Luke 13:11). Their influence can be seen in religious *asceticism, fanaticism* and *false teaching* (1 Tim. 4:1–3). They maintain a constant conflict with believers who seek true spirituality. Demons are the "spiritual hosts of wickedness" they wrestle against (Eph. 6:12, RSV). We must distinguish between demon influence and demon possession. Any sinner may become demon possessed, but a child of God, who may be influenced by demons, is not subject to demon possession since he is indwelt by Christ. Demons are subject to believers through the name of Jesus (Luke 10:17,18). Through him they are more than conquerors over all evil principalities and powers. Demons know, only too well, the eternal fate awaiting them and their prince. When those were cast out of the man living in tombs by Jesus, they pled with him not to torment them before their time (Matt. 8:29; see Matt. 25:41; Rev. 19:20). Under the panoply of God, and by the power of Christ, saints are invincible and can sing with Isaac Watts:

> Should all the hosts of death,
> And powers of hell unknown,
> Put their most dreadful forms
> Of rage and mischief on,
> I shall be safe; for Christ displays
> Superior power, and guardian grace!

7. HIS DOOM

The future of the devil, as well as his past and present history, is to be found in Scripture. After the removal of the true church at the appearance of her glorious Lord, the earth will experience increased satanic activity, through the Beast and the False Prophet. But when Christ comes to usher in his millennial reign, Satan and his two representatives are to be bound and imprisoned for a thousand years. At the end of such a period Satan is released for a little season. Unchanged in character, he will go out to deceive the nations. His freedom comes to an abrupt end when he is taken and cast into the lake of fire (2 Thess. 2:8–10; Rev. 13:2–4; 19:11–20; Matt. 25:41). What a tragic, terrible end for one who had such a privileged beginning. "Into a pit from whose height fallen." Ever conscious of his eternal doom, Satan is determined not to go alone into the abyss with its unrelieved torment. Thus, he ever strives to people hell with as many deluded souls as possible. How grateful we should be if ours is the assurance that we have been wonderfully delivered from the destroying power of Satan.

Our adversary is strong and determined, subtle and insinuating, malicious and designing, active and persevering. He is able to make the world alluring and ensnaring. But as saints we are not ignorant of his treacherous and deceitful services. Our faith rests in him who is greater than Satan. He makes us sharers of his victory over the world, the flesh, and the devil. As we conclude this chapter it may be fitting to ask the question Friday put to Robinson Crusoe: "Why God not kill the devil?"

Since creation, the devil has been a formidable foe owing to his long familiarity with evil. His great hold on humanity may be attributed to the fact that he has assailed every soul since Adam, and age upon age has practiced his deceptive rebellions against God. In his own corrupt heart are all the secrets of hell, and more than ever, with diabolical subtlety and cunning, he exists to destroy the souls and bodies of men. Why, therefore, does God permit his presence and power to continue? With our finite minds this is a question we cannot fully answer.

Free Moral Agents

When God fashioned both angels and men, it was as free moral agents to obey or disobey. As *Lucifer*, Satan used his freedom in the wrong way, as he came to seduce Adam and Eve to do. God could keep Satan and sin out of the world, but this would only leave us as mere machines. Because we were created with freedom of choice between right and wrong, the possibility of sinning was involved in such freedom. Satan and his angels fell from their innocence when they voluntarily rebelled against God. Man was created in innocence but also with freedom of will, and like the hosts of wickedness, he abused his liberty and fell to ruin—and death.

Attainment in Holiness

Contact and conflict with sin is associated with the highest attainment in holiness. In this world of sin and iniquity, it is our combat with Satan that develops spiritual character. We were born again to conquer (John 1:12,13). If there were no foes to fight, no sin to slay, no devil to fear and resist, then life would be devoid of the higher virtue of victory. Thus, God allows his Davids to meet their Goliaths, and by his power they can put the enemy to flight. So, until "the Lord shall consume with the spirit of his mouth," the evil one of his forces, we must fight the good fight of faith.

> Are there no foes for me to face,
>   Shall I not stem the flood?
> Is this vile world a friend to grace,
>   To help me on to God?
>
> Sure I must fight if I would reign,
>   Increase my courage, Lord!
> I'll bear the toil, endure the pain,
>   Supported by Thy Word.

*Now the serpent was more
subtil than any beast of the
field which the Lord God had
made . . . (Gen. 3:1).*

Satan the Antichrist—Before Christ (The Old Testament)

The title of this chapter must not be misunderstood. By it we are not implying that Satan is the fearful *Antichrist* whom John says has yet to come. The prefix, *anti*, means, against, or instead of, and since his fall, Satan has been, not only the enemy of Christ, but conspicuous in usurping his name and rights. Behind all the antichrists and antichristian dogmas through the ages is the arch-adversary of Christ and of his truth. In the main, his satanic efforts have been directed against the Eternal Son, the One to whom he was very near in a past eternity as the mighty Lucifer. This Lucifer was prominent in God's original creation.

It would be enlightening to know just when Satan's animosity toward Christ began. Was it when he learned of God's choice of Jesus as his beloved Son—and of God's plan and purpose through him that jealousy was born in his heart? Was it then that he revolted and sought to become as a God in his own right? Before his fall, as "Lucifer, son of the morning," and as "the anointed cherub," he was near to the throne of God. He must have been cognizant of

God's plan to create a world of sinless, human beings. Did
Satan at that point aspire, in his then unfallen condition, to
seek from God supreme control of such a unique creation?
But when such a request was denied, did he then
determine in his heart to wreck the coming creation?

If this was so, God, as the Omniscient One, discerned
his evil design, and then planned redemption for the
human race. What must not be forgotten is the revelation
that Christ came as the Lamb slain *before* the foundation
of the world. Deliverance, then, from Satan's bondage as
the god of this world, was conceived in a past eternity,
which implies that the cause and need of such a deliverance was foreseen, even before man was created.

As soon as God completed creation with the masterpiece
of man and his partner, Satan commenced to put into
effect the diabolical scheme he had hatched before the first
human pair appeared. With their yielding to his subtle
insinuations as to the Creator's commands, there came the
first announcement in the Bible to Satan himself—of the
coming of One, who, as "the seed of the woman," would
destroy his power and authority. Satan knew, only too
well, who the person would be, born of a woman to thwart
his evil purposes. From that very moment when he heard
his doom pronounced, there began the age-long battle to
destroy the seed from which Christ was to spring. When
he did appear, he tried to destroy him before he died as
God predicted he would. In his death Christ was bruising
his head, or overthrowing his power and authority, which
our Lord did when he cried, "It is finished!" This, then, is
what this chapter is about: Satan's passion to destroy
Christ and his cause, and Christ's conquest over his
adversary, and the provision of salvation for the devil's
dupes in a sin-ridden world.

Having dealt with Satan's preexistence, personality, and
character, we now venture to show that he is portrayed in
Scripture as the great antagonist of our Lord Jesus Christ;

that he bore intense hatred to God's holy and beloved Son from the beginning of his evil career. We name him *the* Antichrist, for all lesser antichrists denying the Father and the Son are energized by Satan himself who leads in rebellion and antagonism toward the Christ who comes to destroy his works. As he is behind all antichristian forces, and the instigator of all open hatred to God, and his Christ, he can be fitly named—

"Satan *the* Antichrist."

Dealing, then, in the first place with the unfolding of Satan's diabolical purpose to checkmate God's redeeming purpose before the Church Period, our minds naturally turn to that portion of Scripture in which the truth of the church, as the body of Christ, is not fully unfolded, namely, the Old Testament.

Although it is true that the Old Testament does not give us an adequate description of the devil's personality and works, yet sufficient is revealed to indicate his determination to block God's promise regarding the sending of his Son into the world as its Savior. And, as we shall see, Satan employed many devices and arts to destroy the "Seed" that would ultimately produce Christ, his great Antagonist and Glorious Conqueror.

1. THE HUMAN RACE

Under this heading we will trace the subtle workings of Satan from the time of Adam to Noah, that is, the primeval period of biblical and human history.

The First Human Pair. Satan's antagonism toward God commenced the moment the Creator sought to people the earth with beings fashioned in his own image. Of course, Satan's own personal revolt and hatred commenced when God deposed him, but in Genesis 3 we have the first recorded attempts of Satan to overthrow the purpose of God regarding man. One writer has pointed out that in each case the human instrument had his own personal interest to serve, while Satan had his own great object in view. Hence God had, in each case, to interfere and avert the evil and the danger of which his servants and people were wholly ignorant.

He Begins with Eve. The first title given to our adversary is highly suggestive, namely, the "serpent" (Gen. 3:1). Here at the very beginning of our Bible, God tears the mask from Satan, revealing him in all his cunning subtlety and cruel deception. He came to Eve with the smooth, covert suggestion of doubt. She had received the divine prohibition regarding "the tree of the knowledge of good and evil" (2:17), but Satan succeeds in bringing Adam's wife under his sway, thus making her the first human sinner in God's restored universe.

He Then Reaches Adam. Because influence is never neutral, Adam quickly succumbs to the subtle purpose of Satan, who through Eve reaches her helpmate, thereby causing the first human pair to fall, thus producing the terrible sorrow and disaster that have marred human lives ever since. So the opening chapter of human history tells us that Satan succeeded in marring not only the angelic harmony, as witnessed by the fall of the angels. He also sowed the seed for the discord that has existed ever since Eden, between God and man.

The Curse and Redemption. With the fall of man, there came the promise of redemption, and it is only as we realize the inner significance of Genesis 3:14,15, where begins "the highway of the *seed*," that we can follow the age-long antagonism between Christ and Satan. In the bruising of the "heel," that is, the lower part, you have the temporary sufferings of the seed; but in the bruising of the "head," that is, the vital part, you have the complete destruction of Satan and his works by Christ, the Victor Divine. Let us linger over two things at this point:

1. The Serpent

In Genesis 3:14, God curses the serpent, that is, the vehicle used by the devil for the accomplishment of his crafty plan. And strange to say, Satan is the first one to receive the promise of redemption. What irony! Now the serpent in his Edenic form is not to be thought of as a writhing reptile. That is the effect of the curse. The creature which lent itself to Satan may well have been the most beautiful as it was the most subtle of creatures less than man. Traces of that beauty remain in spite of the curse. Every movement of a serpent is graceful, and many species are beautifully colored. In the serpent, Satan first appeared as "an angel of light" (2 Cor. 11:14). And the language of verse 14 is easily understood when we remember it is possible that God originally made the serpent with legs. The serpent is the only animal with a long skeleton that goes the length of its body. We also realize the force of the phrase, "it shall bruise thy head," when we keep in mind that the serpent's chief care of itself is for its head, because the heart of the serpent is under its throat.

To the foregoing, we can add that in the curse pronounced against the serpent, sentence was also passed upon the devil himself. The language used betokens his utmost humiliation.

2. The Seed

In this great promise and prophecy of redemption in Genesis 3:15, we have the first link in the long chain of Satan's antagonism. With this gracious word, a window was opened into heaven, and the devil saw, as he had never seen before, something of the matchless grace and boundless love of God.

Knowing something of what the deliverance of man from

sin involved, and that God would preserve the messianic line through the ages until, in the fulness of time, the deliverer should be born of a woman, Satan commenced his enmity against God and man. As soon as his doom was pronounced, he strove in every age and in every way to thwart God's messianic plan of ultimately producing the One from the woman's seed who would utterly and finally destroy the works of the devil.

The First Human Family. It is most interesting to observe how God defeats the crafty purpose of Satan at every point. For example, how disappointed he must have been when he discovered that although God severely punished our first parents, he did not condemn them to the ultimate doom their sin deserved. Judgment was tempered with grace, for in the Promised Seed, all the sons and daughters of Adam's race can find their way back to God.

As Satan's efforts with our first parents failed from the divine standpoint, he speedily concentrated upon their immediate seed and offspring. And so we reach his next stage of antagonism. "Cain rose up against Abel his brother, and slew him" (Gen. 4:8). Abel is a type of the spiritual man. His name, meaning "that which ascends," describes the tenor of his life. The character of his offering in 4:4 made him not only acceptable to God, but also a fitting successor to Adam in the ancestry of our Redeemer.

But Cain slew Abel, and at the back of Cain's anger there was the diabolical antagonism of the devil. Here we have his first attempt to destroy "the seed royal." Was it not this very treacherous act that led our Lord to call him "a murderer from the beginning"? See John 8:44.

But again we find that God not only rules, but overrules, and so to continue the "seed" of Genesis 3:15, Eve bears Seth. "For God, said she, hath appointed me another seed instead of Abel" (4:24–26). Seth, we are reminded, means "substitution." Surely this must have been another reminder to the devil that the substitutionary work of the cross was the weapon God meant to use for his overthrow.

The First Human Generation. Anyone reading Genesis 6 can readily see how the desperation of Satan becomes more intense, and how his hatred is intensified as he discovers that God's omnipotent power is being pitted against him. Through those first centuries of our world's history, his poison spread through the veins of society until we read that "the wickedness of man was great in the earth, and that every imagination of the thoughts of his heart was only evil continually" (6:5). Such an estimation of sin was not from any human standpoint, but from the divine, for it was God who saw.

What desolation and degradation there were! How complete was the ruin of the first generation! "The earth also was corrupt before God, and the earth was filled with violence" (Gen. 6:11). If it be true that "the sons of God" of 6:2 were among "the angels which kept not their first estate," and that their union with "the daughters of man" led to the production of the "mighty men" who evidently were "giants," masters in iniquity and superhuman in size and character, then one can appreciate the solemn word of 6:7, "I will destroy man whom I have created from the face of the earth."

What pleasure must have broken over Satan's evil heart when he heard such a decree! "The end of all flesh is come before me" (Gen. 6:13). Has the arch-foe of mankind succeeded? Is the destruction of "all flesh" going to mean the obliteration of the "seed" God said would bruise his head?

"But Noah"—let us praise the Lord for this blessed "but." God preserved one who was free from the evil of his day. In fact, if the theory of sexual intercourse existing between the fallen angels and the daughters of men which brought about such an abominable corruption and made the Flood an absolute necessity can be true, then the only inference one can draw from the phrase, "Noah . . . perfect in his generations" (Gen. 6:9), is that both he and his family had preserved their pedigree pure from Adam.

With the utter destruction of the antediluvians by the Flood, God defeated the third attempt of Satan to thwart his redemptive purpose, for in preserving Noah both from the corruption of his age, and the judgment falling upon such corruption, God made it possible to continue the seed of the woman that would yet bruise the serpent's head. Reaching Genesis 9, we find God making a fresh start with man upon the earth that had been cleansed and washed by the waters of judgment, from the evil that had stained it. Thus, the curtain falls upon the first period of human history, with its failure on the part of the devil to thwart the supreme counsels of the Lord Most High.

2. The Jewish Nation

The Bible contains a wonderful progress of revelation, as well as of doctrine. Thus, with the opening of Genesis 12, God's gracious scheme for man's deliverance from sin and Satan begins to crystallize. The mighty river is now entering a narrower channel. After the scattering of Noah's sons, nations increased and the earth was replenished, but permeating the life of this new race was the spirit of independence from God. Such a satanic spirit ended in confusion and scattering.

Now for the accomplishment of the promise of Genesis 3:15, God selects from among the nations a people for his own possession. And it is now our purpose to follow the trail of the serpent as he seeks to circumvent God at every turn of the way with his covenant people, the Jews.

The First Jew. Abraham was the first one to be called a "Hebrew" (Gen. 14:13). It was this first Hebrew who received from God the glorious promise of Genesis 12:2–3, in which both Jew and Gentile can participate.

Well, if the purpose of God is to be frustrated, the devil must have Abraham out of the way, so he makes two or three attempts to interfere with the patriarch's seed. The first is found in Genesis 12:10–20, where Satan leads Abraham to forsake the place of blessing, and where, had it not been for God's protection, his wife Sarah would have forfeited the right to bear any seed to Abraham. Turning to Genesis 20, we have a similar failure on Abraham's part. But here again God overrules and Genesis 21 opens with the birth of Isaac, through whom the promise given to Abraham is continued, and from whom Jesus sprang as "the son of Abraham" (Matt. 1:1).

Before leaving Abraham and his kindred, we can turn to Genesis 12:6 and see another subtle attempt to frustrate God: "The Canaanite was then in the land." The promise was: "Unto thy seed will I give this land" (12:7), but the aim of Satan was to occupy Canaan in advance of Abraham and so contest its occupation by his seed.

The First Family. Leaving Abraham, the head of the Jewish race, as he did in the case of Adam, the head of the human race, the devil now turns his attention to the chosen family of Jacob. From Genesis 37 to 50 we have unfolded the great messianic purposes of God. The twelve sons of Jacob, who became the representatives of the twelve tribes of the Jewish nation, fill the pages of this part of Holy Writ.

But in the terrible famine covering the face of the earth (Gen. 41:56), we can detect the next attempt of the "destroyer" to exterminate "the seed of Jacob." And how nearly he succeeded both in the threatened death of young Joseph, and in the subsequent trials which befell him! That Satan was foiled again can be gleaned from Joseph's words after the revelation of himself to his brethren: ". . . ye thought evil against me; but God meant it unto good, to bring to pass, as it is this day, to save much people alive" (Gen. 50:20). In Genesis 45:5, Joseph also speaks about

God sending him on before to preserve life, which means, as indicated in Genesis 45:7, the preserving of a posterity in the earth. Hence the birth of the true Joseph was assured. He is our Zaphnath-paaneah, as Joseph was called in Egypt (Gen. 41:45)—a name meaning "savior of the world."

The Jewish Nation. With the opening of Exodus, we are informed that "the children of Israel [Jacob's divine name (Genesis 32:28), meaning "God commands, orders, or rules"] were fruitful, and increased abundantly, and multiplied, and waxed exceeding mighty; and the land was filled with them" (Exod. 1:7). The Hebrews are now not only a family, but have developed into a mighty nation, mightier even than the Egyptians (Exod. 1:9; Gen. 12:2). Let us now discover the machinations of Satan as he strives to outwit the redemptive plan of God through this chosen nation.

The First Attempt. The "murderer" endeavors, in the first place, to obliterate all the male seed of Israel born in Egypt. What a devilish plan that was, which he put into the heart of Egypt's king, in Exodus 1:15–16. But mark how wonderfully God defeated such a cruel purpose. Those godly Hebrew midwives were his provision and did not accede to Pharaoh's request (Exod. 1:17–20).

When this disappointed, jealous, hard-hearted ruler took matters into his own hands, there were two saintly souls who, because "they were not afraid of the king's commandment" (Heb. 11:23), hid their child, Moses, who, as we all know, became Israel's leader and their mediator both Godward and manward. And let it be noted that the devil overstepped himself, for Pharaoh had to pay for the feeding, the clothing, and the educating of the goodly child on whom Pharaoh's daughter had compassion. As she discovered him, "the babe wept" (Exod. 2:6); and in those tears "lay the defeat of the enemy, the preservation of the nation, the faithfulness of Jehovah's word, the bringing to naught 'the wisdom of Egypt,' and the coming of the seed of the woman." Compare Exodus 1:10 with Job 5:12–13.

The Second Attempt. In his desperation to blot out this chosen nation, Satan is not easily to be discouraged. When we reach Exodus 14, therefore, we find the entire Israelite nation out of the land of Egypt. In verses 11 and 12, however, a bitter complaint is made against Moses. What kind of deliverance was this, when before them was the deep sea, and behind them the chariots of Pharaoh! Truly it was a crucial moment! Is Satan going to succeed in destroying the chosen nation either by slaughter or drowning? Ah, Israel learned that day that it was a real thing to stand still (that was all they could do) and see the salvation of the Lord. No nation or individual is able to fight against the devil, no matter through what Pharaoh he works. "The Lord shall fight for you, and ye shall hold your peace" (Exod. 14:14)—and in the miracle that followed lay Israel's victory and Satan's defeat. Yes, it was God who did it (Ps. 106:9,10).

With the Royal Kingdom. In the course of time, Israel's form of government changed from that of a theocracy, that is, God-ruled, to that of a monarchy, that is, man-ruled. After the death of Moses and Joshua, judges were raised up to guide the affairs of the people, but with the opening of the Book of Samuel, the nation is merged into a kingdom, and Israel, like the surrounding nations, has her throne and king. There is one link in the chain of antagonism during the transitional period of Israel's history to which we can profitably refer. It is found in the Book of Ruth. How disastrous it would have been had Ruth the Moabitess returned to Moab along with Orpah, her sister-in-law, when urged to by Naomi. Had she done so, she would not have become the wife of Boaz, the mother of Obed, the grandmother of Jesse, the great-grandmother of David, and the ancestress of our blessed Lord (Matt. 1:5).

In coming to the kingdom-phase of Satan's antagonism, we believe that he was aware of Jacob's prophetic utterance in Genesis 49:10, that "the sceptre shall not depart

from Judah, nor a lawgiver from between his feet, until
Shiloh come; and unto him shall the gathering of the
people be." Therefore we have in this period of the
kingdom the most thrilling and yet demonic means de-
vised by Satan to break God's word. In drastic ways he
seeks the destruction of "the seed royal," thus severing the
messianic line. We can classify the most prominent assaults of the enemy during the monarchy, united and
divided, as follows:

The Royal Tribe. Coming to 1 Samuel 8:5, we find Israel
demanding a king. Such a request is acceded to, but the
cunning, skillful enemy does all that he can to transfer the
rule or scepter from the tribe of Judah, which, as we have
seen from Genesis 49:10, was the line from which the
Royal One was to spring. The people chose Saul, who was
of "the tribe of Benjamin." Saul's name means "Asked
for." But had the government of Israel been left in
Benjamin's tribe, God's promise of Genesis 49:10 would
have been perverted. And Saul's later career shows clearly
that the Israelites were moved by Satan to appoint him as
king, even as at a later date he moved David to number
Israel. One writer suggests that Saul is a perfect under-
study of Satan: "There is portrayed for us, with great
faithfulness in detail, by the Holy Spirit, the character and
career of a man who fills out, with strange exactness, this
strange story of Satan. It is found in the biography of King
Saul of Israel."

The Royal Seed. With the abandonment of Saul, the
throne of Israel is transferred from Benjamin to Judah (1
Sam. 16). David, a man after God's own heart, is chosen
and anointed king (1 Sam. 16:13; 2 Sam. 2:4; 5:2). And with
such a change, there commences the desperate and
determined attack of Satan upon "the seed royal," that is,
the house of Judah, from which the Messiah must spring.
Let us follow his evil trail, grouping our material around
personalities:

David (1 Sam. 16:13)

Saul, the God-forsaken, Satan-possessed monarch (1 Sam. 16:14), tried his utmost to destroy the Lord's anointed one, and thus David is obliged to flee as a fugitive, hiding in caves and holes from his father-in-law. Three outstanding attempts were made by Saul to slay David, but this sweet psalmist of Israel could sing: "He shall reward evil unto mine enemies; cut them off in thy truth. . . . For he hath delivered me out of all trouble: and mine eye hath seen his desire upon mine enemies" (Ps. 54:5–7). And, as we shall see when we come to great David's greater Son and Lord, these three attempts correspond in some measure to the three attempts Satan made to overcome our Lord, in the wilderness temptations.

Before turning from David's career, however, it may be fitting to observe that he, too, became a tool of Satan. The first mention of Satan in the capacity of an adversary is found in 1 Chronicles 21:1, where we read that "Satan stood up against Israel, and provoked David to number Israel." No wonder God was "displeased with this thing" (1 Chron. 21:7). Puffed up with pride over the number, he might have gone to war and blotted out the 500,000 men of Judah (2 Sam. 24:9).

Jehoram (2 Chron. 21:1–7)

In the union of Jehoram and Athaliah, the daughter of Ahab, king of Israel, Satan continues his assault upon the house of Judah. Jehoram slew all his brethren (v. 4), while he, himself, died of an incurable disease and "departed without being desired" (2 Chron. 21:20). Jehoahaz, v. 17, who is the Ahaziah of 22:1, or Azariah of 22:6, reigned in Jehoram's stead. This ungodly ruler, walking in the evil ways of Athaliah, his mother, is slain along with others of the house of Judah (2 Chron. 22:8).

At this critical moment, God's word appears to be at stake. Those of the royal seed are becoming fewer and fewer. In fact, the light was almost quenched, for Athaliah "arose and destroyed all the seed royal of the house of Judah" (2 Chron. 22:10). What followed? "But Jehoshabeath [another blessed, divine "but" the devil hates], the daughter of the king, took Joash the son of Ahaziah, and stole him . . . [and] hid him from Athaliah, so that she slew him not" (2 Chron. 22:11,12). For six years this cruel queen reigned over Judah, the self-conscious and apparently sole survivor of the royal house, and yet she was not of Judah, but of Israel.

How much depended upon the preservation of Joash! If he dies, then Judah's light and hope will be completely extinguished. Everything depends upon this precious child. Carefully he is hid and cared for while Athaliah reigns on in blissful ignorance until the day dawns when Joash is presented and crowned as king over Judah and Athaliah is slain (2 Kings 11:4–16; 2 Chron. 23:11,15). Thus God, in a marvelous way, defeated the evil tactics of the devil, thereby fulfilling the promise of giving a light forever (2 Chron. 21:7). In summarizing the mischief of Jehoshephat's wrong affinity with Ahab (2 Chron. 18:1), we can trace the enemy's design in breaking into the royal line so as to destroy the promise of Genesis 3:15 and 2 Samuel 7:16. Jehoshaphat made the beginning (2 Chron. 18:1); Jehoram followed it up (2 Chron. 21:4); the Arabians continue the assault (2 Chron. 21:16,17; 22:1); Athaliah nearly succeeds in accomplishing the design of Satan (2 Chron. 22:10).

Hezekiah (Isa. 36:1; 2 Chron. 29:1)

With the continuation of the history of Judah, there is the continuation of the satanic onslaught against the messianic seed within such a royal line. And so we reach another stage of the agelong conflict in the life and service of good King Hezekiah.

1. The First Assault. Satan's first attack is made through the King of Assyria. But Hezekiah, though smitten with fear and sorrow at the boastful taunts of Rabshakeh, "spread it before the Lord" (Isa. 37:14), and God graciously heard his cry and sent forth "the angel of the Lord" to smite the Assyrian host (Isa. 37:36). Truly, deliverance from the devil is wholly of the Lord!

2. The Second Assault. After the attack of the King of Assyria, there came the assault of the king of terrors, even death (Isa. 38:1). According to Hebrews 2:14, Satan had "the power of death" and so, failing to cut off Hezekiah through one monarch, he tries another. Hezekiah, however, turned his face to the wall and prayed, and God, in response to his cry, added fifteen years to his life.

But see how critical the position is. Hezekiah is childless, and, if death conquers, who is there to follow him in the line of Judah? He had no heir to the throne, and in his anxiety he remembers God's word to David in 2 Samuel 7:12–16. Here again the Lord of life intervenes, and three years after Hezekiah's deliverance from death, a son was born to him, Manasseh by name, who became the worst of Judah's kings, as his father had been the best.

THE CAPTIVITY (Esther 3:6)

Judah, the royal tribe, was taken into captivity by Nebuchadnezzar, King of Babylon, but the Book of Esther testifies to God's secret care over his own. Let us continue to follow the assault of Satan against the nation through whom the Seed of the woman was to come.

In seeking the destruction of all the Jews, the devil sought to use Haman, even as he had tried to use Pharaoh in Egypt. In many ways, Haman is a type of the devil. He had power next to that of the king (Esther 3:1). The devil has great might. He could not use that apart from the king's permission (Esther 3:8,9; see John 12:31; 14:30; 16:11; Luke 22:31,32; Job 1:6).

But the sleepless night of the king marked the time for divine action. What God used here to rob Ahasuerus of his rest we do not know, but suffice it to say that he can use small things to accomplish his purpose, as the mighty Goliath learned. With the hanging of Haman, who is called as is no other in Scripture, "the Jews' enemy" (Esther 3:10), and with the exaltation of Esther there came the full emancipation of Judah, and with such, the continuation of God's blessed purpose.

Such a dramatic failure on the part of Satan to overthrow the counsels of God concludes the Old Testament phase of his antagonism. Doubtless in the restoration of the Jews, and throughout the Maccabean Period of four hundred years or more, stretching from Malachi to Matthew, the "destroyer" was untiring in his efforts to thwart the messianic plan. As the time drew near for the coming of the Messiah, the devil must have increased his evil devices to prevent such a glorious advent, just as his rage will be intensified as the second coming of Christ to the earth draws near. But of this we are certain, that against all his satanic attacks in the period for which we have no biblical revelation, there was matched the eternal power of God. If he had succeeded in causing the Old Testament Scriptures to close with the word "curse," such was nothing to boast about. "He who laughs last, laughs longest"—and so the New Testament commences with the name of "Jesus Christ," the One who was coming to bear the curse and destroy the works of the devil.

*The prince of this world is
coming. He has no hold upon
me (John 14:30, NIV).*

Satan the Antichrist—
During and After Christ
(The New Testament)

The opening of the gospel story with the genealogy of
our Lord is of twofold significance. First, we are shown his
connection with the line or house of Judah, from which as
Shiloh, he himself was to spring. For this reason it is
interesting to trace Christ's lineage back to David, as
Matthew does, for the question asked by every Jew of
anyone who claimed to be the Messiah was, "Is he of the
house of David?" So both Matthew and Luke mention
David in their genealogies.

It may be fitting at this point to add a word or two
regarding the difference between these two genealogies as
we have them in Matthew 1 and Luke 3. Matthew traces
the royal succession, thus proving that Jesus Christ was
the Son of David. Luke, on the other hand, gives us the
family lineage and, true to the scope of his Gospel, traces
our Lord's pedigree from the common father of Jew and
Gentile, namely, Adam. And then Matthew differs from
Luke in naming women in the genealogy. Of the four
referred to, three—Tamar, Rahab, and Bathsheba—were
stained with sin. Possibly the purpose of Matthew in

45

recording such characters is to show that he who came to save "that which was lost" did not scorn such descent. As women like these were not excluded from the honor of being in the Messiah's line of ancestry, so others like them would not be shut out from fellowship in his kingdom of grace and love.

For a further insight into the significance of these genealogies, one is referred to a reliable commentary like Ellicott's, where it is easy to prove how the names mentioned in the lists preserved the line of Judah from destruction, until Christ sprang out of Judah, as the Conquering Lion.

The next purpose served by these genealogies is to remind us of the defeat of Satan in his attempts to break the direct messianic line stretching from Adam to Christ. These seemingly dry records of names are a testimony to the fact that all the diabolical methods of the enemy to destroy the house of Judah had miserably failed. Apart from the Old Testament characters we have already mentioned as being specially singled out for satanic assaults, others are mentioned in the genealogies of Matthew and Luke, many of whom, if we but had the full story of their lives, would be found notable as targets for the devil's anti-messianic darts.

Taking up the threads of this absorbing theme of Satan's antagonism to the "seed royal" again, there are two conspicuous periods in which he stands unmasked as the tempter, murderer, liar, prince of demons, adversary, and destroyer.

Before Christ's Birth

As the "Accuser," Satan approached Joseph, the husband of Mary, regarding her pregnant condition. A careful study of Matthew 1:18–25 reveals that Joseph's fear was worked on by the devil. Says one expositor:

The glimpse given us into the character of Joseph is one of singular tenderness and beauty. To him, conscious of being of the house of David, and cherishing messianic hopes, what he heard would seem to come as the blighting of those hopes. He dared not, as a righteous man, take to himself one who seemed thus to have sinned. But love and pity alike hindered him from pressing the law, which made death by stoning the punishment of such a sin (Deut. 22:21; John 8:5), or even from publicly breaking off the marriage on the ground of apparent guilt. There remained the alternative, which the growing frequency of divorce made easy, of availing himself of a "writ of divorcement," which did not necessarily specify the ground of repudiation, except in vague language implying disagreement (Mark 10:4). Thus the matter would be settled quietly without exposure. The "bill of divorcement" was as necessary for the betrothed as for those who were fully man and wife. Now while Joseph "thought on these things," which words suggest a conflict, a perplexity about such a step, the angel of the Lord came, dissolving his doubts and relieving the anxiety of his mind.

So the devil failed with this New Testament Joseph even as he did with his Old Testament namesake. Joseph's pondered action was Satan's assault even as he had assaulted Abraham in Genesis 12:11–13.

After Christ's Birth

If ever the demons had a bad day with their satanic monarch, it was on the day that Jesus was "born of a woman." In the promise that her seed would bruise the serpent's head there lay the hope that God had set before fallen humanity. Throughout the entire array of those who had descended from "the woman," Satan had found no one to fear. But here was a marvel—a child divinely conceived and born. All at once the devil's murderous energies are aroused, and his subtle wisdom used for the attempt to slaughter Mary's infant. Now the utter destruction of Satan and all his evil works depended upon One over whom he had no control, One who was sinless both by birth and practice. And that our Lord was holy by birth is proved by the mention of "her seed." Such a thought as a woman's seed, as stated here, is not found elsewhere. Over a hundred times or more, when we read of the seed and of seeds, of Abraham's seed, and so forth, it is always the *seed of the man*. The *seed of the woman* is a unique concept and can only be interpreted as a foreshadowing of the Virgin Birth, and most remarkable it is that it should be found here. If our Lord had not been born of a virgin, it would have been Adam who would have been addressed, and *his seed* that would have been referred to in Matthew 1:18. In a very true sense, then, the prince of this world had, and consequently found, nothing in the One who sprang from "her seed."

Incidentally, we have a fuller revelation of the cruel machinations of the devil with the coming of Christ, for no one so scathingly portrayed his diabolical character like the Master who had come to destroy his works. He refers to him at least fifteen times, under different names, each of which confirms Satan's personality. It was because Christ knew Satan as no other, that with repeated onslaught, through many agents, he cruelly opposed him throughout his earthly career. When Abraham was called, then he and his seed were bitterly attacked. After David was enthroned, the royal line was constantly assailed. When "the Seed of the woman" himself came, then the storm burst upon him. Thus we come to trace some of the most demonic assaults ever made by the enemy as the roaring lion against an individual, as well as some of his most cunning devices as the angel of light to deceive a trusting soul.

Departure from the Will of God

In his endeavor to entice our Lord away from the revealed plan of God for his life, Satan stands unmasked as

our Lord's fierce rival. In fact, while the Savior was here
below, there were two protagonists in the arena who were
bent on destroying each other's ministry and influence—
the devil, and one "stronger than he." There are at least
three phases of this bitter conflict between God's adversary and God's Son:

1. The Temptation in the Wilderness (Matt. 4:1-11)

At the very outset of the Master's public ministry he was
brought face to face with the devil. Fresh from the divine
approval at Jordan, he encountered the diabolical antagonism of him who is here named "the devil" for the first
time in the Gospels. If there is no devil, then there is no
Christ, for both are represented as speaking to each other.
It is not our present purpose to enter into all the details of
Satan's daring attempt to make Christ a sinner. A short
word on each temptation will suffice.

In the *first temptation* to make bread out of stones, it is
not difficult to pick up the satanic trail. Satan wanted
Christ to assert his own power, and thus satisfy a natural
need. If he was the Son of God, did that not involve
lordship over nature? Then why not make bread out of the
loaflike flints of the Jordan desert and thereby appease the
pangs of hunger? With this first exercise of miraculous
power of which he was the conscious possessor, he would
establish his *status* as the Messiah in the eyes of the Jews.

But such a putting forth of his power, although legiti-
mate when hungry crowds must be fed, would have been
an act of self-assertion and distrust on the Savior's part. It
would have involved not the affirmation, but the denial of
the Sonship which had so recently been attested. If his
Father had given him a work to do, he would sustain him
until its completion. Further, Jesus always used his power
for others, never for himself.

In the *second temptation* Christ is taken to the pinnacle
of the temple and told to cast himself down. In this subtle

suggestion Satan desires Christ to test his attestation that he was the beloved Son. What a crucial experience of Sonship!

By such a sudden appearance in the temple, Christ would obtain power and popularity, and as to the possibility of destroying himself in descending, had not God promised angelic guardianship? But this attempt of Satan to identify Christ with vainglory, spectacular popularity, and distrust is thwarted by the Savior. The derivation of the tempter's name is worthy of repeating at this point. *Devil* is derived from *diabolus*—*dia* meaning "down"; *ballo*, "to throw." So he is well named, as "thrower-down." Someone has said: "The Devil *throws down;* the blessed Savior *lifts up*." But this second attempt to destroy Christ is foiled.

In the *third temptation* Satan's pretensions are very clear. He now addresses his temptation not to the sense of Sonship, but to the love of power. To be a king, like other kings, mighty to deliver his people from their oppressors, and achieve the glory which the prophets had predicted for Christ—this was possible for him only if he would go beyond the self-imposed limits of accepting whatsoever his Father ordered for him.

Satan's purpose is apparent. He is "the god of this world" and will not allow any relationship to the true God. Satan's attitude of pretense is often the same as the attitude of a pretender to the throne—he claims it as his right. That our Lord recognized the devil's right to the kingdom of this world is evident from the fact that three times over he alluded to him as its "prince" (John 12:31; 14:30; 16:11), while Paul refers to his hosts as "the rulers of the darkness of this world" (Eph. 6:12). But he is a usurper prince, because Christ is the Prince of Kings, of Life, of Peace (Rev. 1:5; Acts 3:15; Isa. 9:6). As crafty Absalom stole the hearts of King David's subjects, so Satan is out to rob God of his own. "Fall down and worship me"—what arrogant assumption and blatant self-importance! What naked and absolute antagonism to the divine will!

Look at Christ's treatment of the tempter at this final stage—"Get thee hence." What an assertion of divine power and authority even over the devil! "Leave!" Jesus did not ask him, politely, to go; he commanded him to retreat. The encouraging thing for our hearts is the fact that Satan obeyed.

Before closing this section of our meditation, it will be found profitable to contrast the two initial assaults of the devil. The first Adam failed to overcome Satan in a garden—the Last Adam succeeded. The circumstances of each tempted one were different. Adam had a wife by his side—Christ was alone. Adam's conflict was in a garden—Christ's in the wilderness. Adam had plenty of food around him—Christ was hungry. Adam had safety among the trees—Christ was surrounded by wild beasts.

May ours be the resolute determination to make our Lord's glorious victory over the devil more actual in our own lives!

2. The Clamor for Kingship (John 6:15)

There may be another evidence of Satan's purpose to side-track Christ from his work as Redeemer in the above portion, where the populace, after the miracle of the loaves, sought by force to carry him to the royal city and acclaim him as their temporal king. But such a shortcut to the throne would have been a direct departure from the will of God, namely, that the Savior was to reach his throne via the tree. "I, if I be lifted up . . . will draw all men unto me" (John 12:32). We have to learn, even as the devil did when Christ by evading the crowd turned his back on a crown, that there are no quick, easy steps up to God's throne. "To him that overcometh will I grant to sit with me in my throne" (Rev. 3:21).

3. The Easier Path (Mark 8:31,32)

Here we have another insight into Satan's subtle attempts to lead Christ astray. Peter is startled as our Lord unfolds many of the terrible experiences ahead to which he will yield, and with impetuous speech, he blurts out, "Be it far from thee" (Matt. 16:22). Peter wanted his Lord to gain a kingdom without sacrifice, and victory without suffering, a crown without a cross. This warm-hearted yet impulsive disciple did not realize that just as God had lifted him up and blown a blast, as a trumpet, through him regarding Christ's deity (which Jesus recognized as the voice of the Father), so now Satan is taking him up and blowing a different blast through him. But Jesus quickly detected the satanic suggestion and identified Peter's desire to have his Master pity himself as being from Satan, whose first beginnings of deception are along the line of self-pity.

Notice how Christ meets the tempter. He rebuked Satan as being in Peter, and he said to Peter, "Get thee behind me, Satan . . ." (Mark 8:33). And the sharpness of the reply indicates a strong and intense emotion. The devil is spoken to by Christ as in the wilderness, for this approach was nothing less than a renewal of the same temptation. He desired Christ to gain his crown without the cross—to draw back from the path which the Father had appointed for him. And so, knowing that Calvary was the only fulfilment of the redemption promise of God in Genesis 3:15, Christ turns from Satan with the stinging rebuke, "Thou art an offense unto me" (Matt. 16:23).

PREMATURE DEATH

Departure from God or death before the cross—such was the devil's double-barrelled gun, loaded against Christ.

For thousands of years Satan had laughed at God's

redemptive scheme, ridiculing and scorning the hope embodied in the pronouncement in the garden, but God was not upset or alarmed about the final issue. It was "impossible for him to lie"; therefore, in spite of all the efforts of Satan to block his own deserved defeat, Christ came according to promise. And from the moment of his miraculous birth, the "destroyer's" great passion was to give Christ a speedy exit. As "the power of death" was still in his hands, he endeavored in various ways to bring the Lord of Life to a premature death. Let us mark several of his murderous approaches.

(a) *The Herods*. If, as we have noted, the Old Testament presents us with fitting types of Satan in Saul and Haman, then in the New Testament also we can detect human personifications of the devil's subtlety and cruelty.

Herod the Great (Matt. 2:1–23). There is a certain correspondence between the tactics employed against the promised "seed" in the Old Testament and the actual "Seed" in the New Testament. For example, in the case of Joseph in Matthew 2, there was the crafty work of doubt and suspicion, as in the case of Eve in Genesis 3. Then with the introduction of both family and national life, the devil stands out branded like Cain as a "murderer," for the slaughter of Abel, and then of the male children of Israel through Pharaoh, was conceived in his murderous heart. Here in the New Testament, Herod becomes the tool of Satan in the cruel massacre of the innocents, the number of which, if the population of Bethlehem was about two thousand at that time, did not exceed thirty in all. Let it not be forgotten that the first martyrs for Christ's sake were these children of Rachel.

Had the innocent Child Jesus been among the lowly band of sufferers, what a dark day it would have been for the world. But the devil did not succeed, for just as God intervened in the sparing of Moses, so Joseph and Mary through the medium of a dream defeated the cunning plan of Herod, which was but the product of Satan's cruel mind. Divine interposition was needed to outwit the designs of the enemy; and guidance was given to our Lord's guardians only as and when needed (Matt. 2:19–21).

But further, suppose Christ had been among those dear babies doomed to die. Herod would not have succeeded, for Mary's helpless Babe was "the mighty God," and, as the Sinless One, premature death such as the devil planned for him could have no claim upon him.

Herod Antipas (Luke 13:31–35). "Herod will kill thee"— what startling words these are! Our Lord's answer, "Go ye, and tell that fox," favors the idea that the Pharisees had been sent by this Herod, the son of Herod the Great, to announce his purpose as a threat. It is true that in Luke 23:8 we are told that this self-same Herod was "desirous of seeing him of a long season," but oscillations of vague curiosity and vague fears were quite in keeping with the tetrarch's character. The answer of Christ is the only word of unmitigated contempt recorded among the utterances of our Lord. Such a reply was more than justified by the mingled tyranny and timidity, insolence and baseness of Herod Antipas. "Go ye, and tell that fox." This word was eminently descriptive of the character of this Herod, and of the whole Herodian house. For example, in the previous Herod you have the craftiness of the man in the guise of a worshiper of the very One he desired to slay.

Says Ellicott: ". . . the fact that the Greek word for 'fox' is always used as a feminine, gives, perhaps, a special touch of indignant force to the original. He had so identified himself with Herodias that he had lost his manliness, and the proverbial type of the worst form of woman's craft was typical of him."

What courage and fearlessness our blessed Lord displayed! Herod "hoped to have seen some miracle done by him" (Luke 23:8), and Jesus, reading his thoughts, tells him that the time for such sights and wonders was all but over. "I do cures today and tomorrow, and the third day I shall be perfected" (Luke 13:32). In effect, our Lord's reply to Herod's threat means, "I shall stay in Herod's dominion with perfect security for a brief while longer, till my work is done." And walk and work he did until his miraculous ministry was completed with the crowning miracle at Bethany (John 11:40–44).

Poor Herod—he was but the devil's tool! His foxlike character, reflected in the knavish craftiness of the Pharisees, was a gift of Satan. Beyond the desire of Herod to kill Jesus we can discern the cunning plan of Satan to bring Christ to an untimely end. But into the death-purpose of the devil, Christ flings the word, "I must walk today, and tomorrow and the day following" (Luke 13:33). In spite of the devil and his host of demons, Christ as "The King Immortal" was "immortal until His work was done."

(b) *The Pharisees*. Christ's agelong antagonist had no more willing confederate in his diabolical purpose to bring our Lord to a speedy end than the Pharisees and the Sadducees, who, although it may sound ironical, were the most strictly religious people of Christ's day. Let the following passages stand out in all their grim nakedness:

"And consulted that they might take Jesus by subtilty, and kill him" (Matt. 26:4); "took counsel . . . how they might destroy him" (Mark 3:6); "led him unto the brow of the hill whereon their city was built, that they might cast him down headlong" (Luke 4:29); "ye seek to kill me" (John 8:37); "then took they up stones to cast at him" (John 8:59; 10:31–39).

What happened as the result of these repeated attempts upon our Lord's life? Why, he appeared to possess a "charmed life," for he could pass through all these murderous intentions, as the Hebrew youths did through the fiery furnace, wonderfully preserved by God (Ps. 2:2–4; Dan. 3:26,27).

(c) *The Storms.* In the striking narratives of Matthew 8:23–27 and Mark 4:37–41, we are given another sphere of the devil's activity. By the employment of the word "behold," our attention is called to another stage of the bitter conflict. As the "prince of the power of the air," Satan was responsible for whipping up the sea into fury, thus endangering the lives of all within the boat. The fearstricken disciples did not know they were wrestling, not against wind and storm, but against evil forces using such means in their attempt to cause the death of the sleeping Master. How did Christ meet this satanic assault? The more literal reading of his words, "rebuked the wind, and said unto the sea, Peace, be still," is immensely suggestive: "He said unto the sea, Lie down, be muzzled." It is the sort of language one uses in speaking to a dog that is misbehaving. If a word be repeated in a sharp, peremptory tone of command, in which we speak to a dog, it makes the sense yet more intense and real: "Down, sir! Lie down! Shut up!"

This whole passage is significant. It is not the sort of language to be used in talking merely to wind and wave, especially by a Man evenly poised, as our Lord was. There is, at once, the recognition of an evil spirit, or a group of them, who had aroused an unusually violent storm.

The very language used is a recognition of personality. There was someone at work through wind and water. He is ordered down. He obeys. There ensues a great calm. But the point to mark just now is that Satan's sphere of action includes wind and water as well as the earth. Mark keenly observes why this is the sphere of his activity—because we are here. As he was after Christ, so he is after those of us who are Christ's, and through us, the dominion of this realm.

(d) *The Gethsemane Conflict*. That the agony in the garden marked a further stage in Satan's antagonism toward Christ is shown in the accounts of Gethsemane (Matt. 26:38,39; Luke 22:53; John 18:1–11). "This is your hour, and the power of darkness" (Luke 22:53) declared our Lord as he emerged from the garden. A striking evidence of a satanic assault is seen in the fact that angelic ministration was given as soon as the conflict was over, as in the wilderness conflict (Luke 22:43).

Why did our Lord sweat great drops of blood? What is the meaning of his cry, "Oh my Father, if it be possible, let this cup pass from me!" Surely this request did not mean that he was beginning to shrink from the cross, and that he wanted this "cup" kept from him. Had he not already declared his willingness to drink of the cup given him by his Father? And did he not know that Calvary was the climax of his pilgrimage here below; and that for such a death his face was steadfastly set toward Jerusalem? Did he not declare his delight to do the will of God, even though he knew that God's will was the cross with all its shame and agony?

What, then, is the explanation of his cry of anguish in Gethsemane? Simply this, that he, overcome with extreme physical weakness and suffering, wondered whether he could hold out until the cross was reached. His spirit was willing to tread every inch of the blood-red way to Calvary, but his flesh was so weak. His soul was "crushed with anguish to the very point of death," as Dr. Weymouth translates Matthew 26:38—and so the phrase we misapply to ourselves is identified with Christ, "My spirit—my body."

Having the power of death, it was Satan's passion to get Christ out of the way before the cross. Previous attempts had failed, as we have seen. Is he to succeed in the garden? No, the cup of physical weakness was taken from him, for an angel came and strengthened the Savior; and rising from the bloodstained dust, he passes out of the garden, a victor over the foe. Christ emerged from the garden miraculously empowered for the final onslaught. He has one death to die—the death of the cross.

(e) *Calvary*. It is perfectly true that the devil was indirectly responsible for the death of Christ (seeing he was bearing the curse pronounced upon man for his disobedience in listening to the satanic voice). Yet, directly, the devil tried his utmost to prevent Jesus from going to the cross, since his death thereon was the fulfillment of the redemptive promise and prophecy of Genesis 3:15, and also the death-knell of the devil and his works. Someone has said, "Through death he rendered powerless him who had authority over death, that is, the devil." Such a death was the last thing Satan desired. He was anxious for Christ to die *before* the cross, but not *on* the cross. This death differed from all other deaths. Others *suffer* death; Christ *achieved*. To others, death comes to frustrate their work. Christ's death consummated, crowned and completed his work. It was on the cross he uttered that triumphant cry, "It is finished." The death and resurrection of Christ were his greatest work, his supreme act, his most glorious achievement—hence, the devil's purpose to block and prevent it.

The Jews have a legend that Satan accuses men day and night, the whole year round, except on the day of atonement, and then he is utterly silenced. Surely this testifies to what the enemy of souls thinks of the cross!

God's adversary and ours did not want Christ to stay on his cross and utter, not as a poor, emaciated man with a weak, failing voice, but as a Mighty Victor conscious of achieving an eternal conquest over all satanic forces, the cry, "It is finished!" This can be proved by the fact that he sought every possible way to persuade Christ to leave his cross. Read the accounts of the crucifixion and you will find that the rulers, priests, people, and thieves, all alike, urged Christ to come down from the tree and save himself. But a Christ without his cross is unthinkable.

Behind such pleading voices there can be detected both the desperation and the subtlety of Satan. Had Jesus exercised his own power, and descended, we should have been of all men most miserable. But, marvel of marvels, he stayed there! Hallelujah, what a Savior! The glory of the gospel is wrapped up in this sublime truth, that poor and weak though we be in this sublime truth, that poor and weak though we be in ourselves, and no match whatever for the devil, yet we have the prerogative of overcoming him through the blood of the Lamb. Yes, and let it never be forgotten that Christ refused the myrrh that could deaden the consciousness of his anguish. He determined to die sublimely conscious that he was a glorious Victor, and not a poor, emaciated victim. Calvary was to be the devil's Waterloo, and he knew, and knows it now!

(f) *The Grave*. For Satan's next move, we turn to Matthew 27:62–66. Christ has died and is buried. If the adversary could not prevent him from dying on the cross, then he must endeavor to keep him dead, seeing that his resurrection would be but God's receipt for the debt paid at Calvary. Having a faint knowledge of the far-reaching influence of the Resurrection, Satan makes his last great attempts to destroy God's magnificent and perfect plan of redemption. So the sepulchre is made sure, the stone sealed, and a watch or guard set. No doubt all the empire of Satan rang with triumphant shouts, peal on peal, as the spirit of Jesus passed out of his body into Paradise. But little did they realize that in his death and burial Christ had passed completely out of Satan's power. The devil knew it—he knew it only too well.

Those who thirsted for the blood of Christ might have said:

> Now he is dead! Far hence he lies
> In the lone Syrian town,
> And on his grave, with shining eyes,
> The Syrian stars look down.
>
> *Matthew Arnold*

But the Christian's song is of a different strain—"Death could not keep its prey." On the third day the tomb was emptied of the dead body, and our Lord arose "a Victor o'er the dark domain." So the devil's attempt to keep Christ's body sealed in the tomb was defeated.

Then followed the other half of this last assault against the Lord's Anointed. When the Chief Priests learned of Christ's Resurrection, they resorted to a lie, for the soldiers who kept guard were bribed to say that his disciples had come by night and stolen his body. In their blindness the soldiers failed to see that such a concocted story was a bad testimony in respect to their vigilance. Anyhow, the lie caught on and was believed among the Jews.

Our Lord declared that, in the days of his flesh, the devil was a liar, "for he is a liar, and the father of it" (John 8:44), and true to his character, the devil scattered this fabrication about the empty tomb.

(g) *The Resurrection.* "Whom God hath raised up" (Acts 2:24)—and this the devil knew full well, as did also the "five hundred brethren" (1 Cor. 15:6). "It was not possible that he should be holden of it" (Acts 2:24). Why not possible? Because he was God as well as man. Because the Scripture cannot be broken. Because it is unthinkable that the devil and death should triumph. Not only did he rise again as he had said he would, but he ascended up on high (Acts 1:1–11). In his ascension he passed triumphantly through the realm of the "spiritual hosts of evil, arrayed against us in the heavenly warfare." Having ascended above "the Prince of the Power of the Air," he now makes over to his blood-washed ones the blood-bought victory of Calvary over all the wiles of the devil. Like another Joash, he is *seated* and *expecting* (Heb. 10:12,13), hidden in the house of God on high, and the members of "the one body" are hidden there "in God" (Col. 3:1–3), like another Jehosheba; and going forth to witness of his coming like another Jehoiada (2 Chron. 23:3).

So we have reached the end of the second round in this grim contest between Satan and God, hell and heaven, darkness and light, and the Lord Jesus Christ is still the Victorious One. In the Old Testament Satan tried to prevent the "Seed" from living, and when dead, from rising; but God compassed his Son about with songs of deliverance. Now as the triumphant Lord, he can comfort our devil-beset hearts with the words, "Fear not; I am the first and the last; I am he that liveth, and was dead; and, behold, I am alive for evermore, Amen; and have the keys of hell and of death" (Rev. 1:17,18).

*. . . as ye have heard that
antichrist shall come, even
now are there many anti-
christs; whereby we know that
it is the last time (1 John 2:18).*

Satan the Antichrist—
Present and Future

Cognizant of the fact that Christ had promised to build his church, Satan continues his age-long antagonism. Having failed to destroy Christ, every effort must be made to annihilate what Christ came to produce. The reason, therefore, for Satan's unabated hatred and opposition to the corporate church and to the individual members of such is his desire to injure Christ through his body, the church.

DURING THE CHURCH PERIOD

Because the church was brought into being to continue the redemptive ministry of her risen and glorified Head, she must be destroyed in some way or another. Her message must be nullified and her witness made of none effect. Thus, in this church-age, Satan is striving to thwart and destroy the influence of Christ and of Christian teaching through the church. In spite of the fact that Christ declared that the gates of hell can never prevail against his church, the devil yet works untiringly for her overthrow. The reason for his unabated hatred and opposition is twofold.

There is:

1. The Miracle of Regeneration

It may be that Satan strove to keep Jesus from the cross seeing that he possibly knew Calvary would result in Pentecost. By the Holy Spirit in the work of regeneration, we are made partakers of Christ and of the divine nature. Being indwelt by Christ, the conflict is transferred from Christ to ourselves.

In our unregenerate state, there was no antagonism. Satan was our god, and, being under his sway, we encountered no opposition. Being born anew, however, meant that we were immediately brought into contact with heavenly forces, and made to realize that such would be opposed by demonic powers.

2. The Ministry of Reconciliation

In the days of the early church, Satan made a desperate bid to strike at Christ, the Head, through Christians, the members of his body. Thus, as Satan moved David to number Israel, in like manner he moved Saul of Tarsus to slay all those naming the name of Christ. With authoritative letters from Damascus he, breathing out threatenings and slaughter against the disciples, whether they were men or women, determined to stamp out all who were of Christ, the Way (Acts 8:1–5).

That Saul of Tarsus, all unconsciously, was attacking Christ through his disciples is clearly seen in our Lord's reply to Saul's question: "I am Jesus whom thou persecutest" (Acts 9:5). The proposed slaughter of the disciples was really a blow struck at Christ. Through Saul, then, Satan was seeking to wipe out the testimony of the cross and the Resurrection, knowing as he did that the preaching of such would cause his kingdom to totter in many a life. Over 500 brethren had seen the Risen Lord and every effort must be made to exterminate them, hence Satan's inspiration of Saul in his passion to slaughter the disciples.

The Lord, however, not only rules, but overrules. He can make the wrath of man to praise him, as is evident by Saul's conversion. Once the tool of the enemy, he lived to become the greatest opponent, next to Christ, that the devil ever had. Once his eyes were opened to the reality of the power of hell, his gifted pen never rested until, by means of his letters, he thoroughly unmasked the diabolical designs of Satan. The mighty labors of the apostle Paul must have produced constant anger in the courts of his satanic majesty. This was the man who, in spite of demons and men, could lay down his task confident that he had kept the faith.

The Early Church

The Acts of the Apostles and the Epistles are not only a record of what the Holy Spirit made possible through the apostles, they also contain a valuable contribution to Satan's record as the cruel antagonist of Christ and his own. Let us enumerate some of the methods he adopted to ruin the testimony of the Church in the early days of its existence.

Severe Persecution

Commencing with Saul's ambition to slaughter the disciples, Satan appears to have been tremendously active in the days when the church had power to turn the world upside down.

What battles for the Lord those early disciples had to wage! What terrible persecutions were theirs! Early church history reveals the horrible ways by which the devil, as the murderer, sought to exterminate the saints. Many perished for Christ's sake; but, as ever, the blood of the martyrs is the seed of the church. Thus, in spite of the rage of hell, the testimony goes on.

Hindered Service

A close study of Paul's Epistles convinces one of Satan's reality as a person. To the apostle he was not only an evil force, but a personality, subtle, cruel and persistent. It is Paul who acquaints us with the fact that one of the clever disguises of Satan is that of a hinderer. No matter what the outward circumstances were which prevented the apostle from visiting the Thessalonians, he knew that Satan had hindered him (1 Thess. 2:18).

Great doors of opportunity confronted Paul, but with them there was the adversary. Conflicts with men were his, but Paul knew that his seen foes were only the tools of the unseen arch-foe. Did he not confess that he wrestled not merely against flesh and blood, but against Satan and his wicked host?

Being the greatest exponent of Christ and his gospel the church has ever known, all hell would have gone on holiday if Paul had remained blind or been killed in the early days of his witness.

False Teaching

A casual reading of the Epistles, Pauline and general, reveal how Satan tried to wreck the testimony and influence of the church through the propagation of false teaching. Men arose who mixed truth with error—they departed from the faith; they turned to fables; they denied the Lord who had bought them. Paul, the wonderful founder of churches, came to the end of his days a broken-hearted man as he viewed the ravages of Satan in some centers he had been used of the Lord to create. And, realizing that after his departure another gospel than that he had so faithfully preached would be prevalent, he ceased not to warn the flock, and that with tears, of the coming apostasy.

Unholy Living

There is nothing that can ruin the influence of the gospel like the inconsistency of those who have embraced it. Thus Satan leaves no stone unturned in his endeavor to sidetrack the saints. What tragedies he is responsible for! What a poignant passage that is in the Philippian Letter where Paul speaks of those who once walked by the same rule, but whose earthiness cost him so many tears. Once professed friends, they had become enemies of the cross of Christ (Phil. 3:17–19).

The devil knows only too well that sin or worldliness in the life of a believer stabs Christ in the back. As the embodiment of evil, Satan hates holiness and seeks thereby to cripple the cause of Christ through unsanctified living. A holy life is Christ's most powerful weapon against the evil one and all unholy forces.

Physical Weakness

In the days of his flesh, the Master was active and fruitful in his resistance to the devil. It was the Holy Spirit who, occupying the body of our Lord, made it the medium of defeat for the devil, and of blessing for his dupes. Apart from weariness, the physical weaknesses afflicting our bodies had no place in his sinless body.

In the story of the woman loosed from her infirmity the Master teaches us to believe that Satan was responsible for this woman's physical misery and bondage: "This woman . . . whom Satan hath bound, lo, these eighteen years" (Luke 13:10–16). Paul likewise referred to his physical disability as a messenger of Satan to buffet him (2 Cor. 12:7). If Satan then can get at our bodies (and, in the old nature, he has a vantage point from which to work), we can expect him to incapacitate us for service in some way or another. Of course there are times when sickness is permitted by God that he might be glorified. Saints, however, through lack of care and forgetful of the fact that the body is the temple and channel of the Holy Spirit, often lay themselves open to the attack of the devil along the avenue of the physical. Once he succeeds in incapacitating the mind or body, he has set in motion those influences destructive to a Spirit-filled, inspired witness.

It may be profitable, at this point, to briefly summarize the teaching of Scripture on the appearance, nature and condemnation of all those who are antagonistic to Christ and his Word. The idea of antichrist pervades Scripture, although in the Old Testament assailants exhibit opposition to the Father rather than to his anointed Son. Yet both are objects of satanic assaults. "The kings of the earth have set themselves, and the rulers take counsel together, *against* the Lord, and against his Anointed" (Ps. 2:2,3).

Then, as we discover in the Gospels, the activity of Satan is directed, principally against Christ. In his discourse on future events he warned his disciples against "False Christs" and "false prophets," who would arise to deceive, even the elect (Matt. 24:15, 24; Mark 13:22). The temptation represents the conflict between Christ and the chief antichrist. How it grieved him when his miracles were attributed to the power of his avowed enemy (Matt. 12:24–32).

The Epistles present a fuller revelation of the machinations of the forces of Belial (2 Cor. 6:15). It is Paul who gives us the cameo of Christ's adversary as "The Man of Sin," whom the Lord is to slay by the breath of his mouth (2 Thess. 2:3–9). Then John, who alone uses the term *antichrist* in Scripture, devotes several passages to the antichristian forces at work among the saints of his time, as well as in the ages to come. The spirit of antichrist was prevalent in apostolic times. Says the apostle, "Even now are there many antichrists; whereby we know that it is the last time" (1 John 2:18).

An antichrist is one who denies the Father and the Son, and also the Incarnation (1 John 2:22,23; 4:3; 2 John 7). A characteristic feature of his work is that of *deceit*. "This is a deceiver and an antichrist" (2 John 7). Such an apostate deceiver never belonged to Christ (1 John 2:19; 4:2,3). "The spirit of antichrist" is that which characterizes one embraced in such a category, namely, the unashamed denial of Jesus as God manifest in flesh (1 John 4:3).

The "many antichrists" John speaks of precede and prepare the way for the coming of *the* Antichrist. The apostle says, "Ye have heard that antichrist shall come" (1 John 2:18). This dread person is to be distinguished from all other apostates for he is "the beast . . . out of the earth," the visible manifestation of Satan (Rev. 13:11), appearing during "The Great Tribulation." He is not a revelation of Satan, in his own evil person, but his spawn through whom he fulfils himself in and through on the earth, as a potentate who arrogates to himself divine honors. The king of Babylon and the prince of Tyre foreshadow the Beast, Satan's tool (Isa. 14:4; Ezek. 28:2).

The doom of this most terrible tyrant, Satan's willing instrument of wrath against God and the Jewish saints, along with that of his false prophet, is certain (Rev. 19:20). Since apostolic times, antichrists have been sought in historical persons. Early Protestants saw in the pope and papacy the antichrist. After the Reformation, the papacy saw in Martin Luther and the Reformed Church, the antichrist. Satanic attacks upon Christ and the Christian truth and upon Christians themselves are numerous today, and it is our prayer for spiritual wisdom to detect the wiles of the devil, and, by divine grace, to shun them.

> Christian, seek no yet repose,
>   Hear thy gracious Saviour say,
> Thou art in the midst of foes;
>   Watch and pray.
>
>   *C. Ellicott*

THE PRESENT-DAY CHURCH

One is skipping over the intervening years, stretching from the first century to the twentieth. With church history as our guide, we can travel from the days of the early Fathers to the dark middle ages with their terrible persecutions in the name of religion, and from such to the present time, and mark the slimy trail of the serpent. Behind the rise of the papacy and the horrors associated with it, we can detect the sinister figure of Satan. Fascinating, however, as this phase is, from the standpoint of the student, let us look at things as they are, to discover if Satan's hostility toward Christ and his church is as fierce as ever. Has time mellowed him? Have the setbacks he has experienced robbed him of his sting? Has he changed? Changed! Not a bit of it! He is just as much the devil as he ever was.

Yes, and a devil he must remain. The saints are to have a new name, but not so the devil. His name and his diabolical nature are as deathless as himself. His tactics may change, and they do, with each succeeding generation, but Satan himself cannot change.

If anything, he is worse now than he ever was. Having a faint idea of prophecy, he knows that his time is short, and with accelerated speed he is pursuing his deadly task. Marshalling all his demoniac forces together, as he is, for a final onslaught against Christ and his anointed, we can expect intense antagonism in this, our day and generation.

1. Modern Heresies

That Satan can be a very religious devil is proven by what the apostle Paul has to say about him transforming himself into "an angel of light." His manifestation, and we have to face this fact, is not the gruesome representation of a fork-carrying person having horns and a tail, but a satanically religious manifestation, subtle and disastrous in its working.

For the last sixty or so years professors and teachers in centers of theological training have had Satan's special attention, and so successful has he been that modernism has thoroughly penetrated the church. His ministers—yes, the devil's ministers, for he has many in the ministry!—are masquerading as ministers of truth and righteousness.

Modernism, we hold, is the creation of hell, no matter how religious it may seem to be. Modern heresies and criticism are pitted against the infallible Word, the infallible Christ, the fact of sin, the redemptive works of the cross, the witness of the Holy Spirit. Knowing how completely the deity and death of Christ destroyed his works, Satan, through religious teachers, has been attacking the virgin birth, the sinlessness, the efficacious death, and the resurrection of our blessed Lord. Modernists have taken away our Lord and we know not where they have laid him.

By modernism, Satan has succeeded in robbing the church of her power in the world. With a humanized Christ, a mutilated Bible, and a glorified self, modernism is bankrupt. Nothing can damn evangelism like modernism, and Satan knows that—hence his untiring efforts to create an ever-increasing army of false teachers. My soul, come not nigh their dwelling (see 2 Cor. 11:13–15). Let us pray for spiritual perception, whereby we can detect, and that immediately, the subtle error in a good deal we hear from some of the pulpits of our land.

The Scribes and Pharisees of old were blatantly anti-Christ while he lived and labored among them. How fierce were their attacks upon his works and words! Such was their persistent antagonism toward him that he called them "children of the devil," though they pretended to be highly religious. Since their day Christ has been repeatedly wounded in the house of reputedly religious people, the

most recent stab in his back coming from seven theologians in a book called *The Myth of God Incarnate*,
published by the SCM Press, London. The central thesis
of this further attack upon the deity of Jesus is that we
should cease to think and speak of him as God-made-flesh,
as John distinctly declares he was (John 1:1, 14).

The suggestion made by these seven *apostates*, as they
actually are, is that we must accept Jesus only as a man
approved of God as a divinely inspired teacher. The
professor of divinity at Oxford opens the book with a
chapter on "Can there be a Christianity without Incarnation?" He then goes on to assert there can be. But if there
were no Incarnation, there would be no Christianity,
which is *supernatural* religion. Since Christ's day, his life
has been regarded as a decisive act of God in human
history.

In spite of their attacks on the foundational truths of the
Christian faith, each of the seven theologians emphatically
state that they are Christians. John, however, writing of
those who deny that Jesus was God manifest in flesh,
called such deniers *liars* (1 John 5:10). These Anglican
leaders not only attack the incarnation of Jesus, but also his
resurrection, affirming that we should not regard it as an
actual physical fact, but only as an emotional experience.
Such heresy portrays Jesus as a liar, for he often declared
that he would rise again from the dead, which he did. "I
was dead, and, behold! I am alive for evermore." There
was also the apostolic witness of his resurrection.

A further dastardly attack upon the veracity of Jesus
comes at the end of *The Myth of God Incarnate* in which
the writer says, "To prove an historical negative such as
the sinlessness of Jesus is notoriously difficult to the point
of impossibility. . . . We must admit that we have not
evidence enough to guarantee the self-consistency of
Jesus." How can men call themselves *Christians* when
they reject our Lord's own testimony as to his sinlessness:

"Which of you convinceth me of sin?" (John 8:46). How Satan must laugh over the full-blooded skepticism of the New Testament that flows incessantly through the essays of these religious scholars! The seven men who wrote these words have no right to be in the *Christian* ministry, receiving pay from the *Christian* church.

Further, how blind they are to the fact that their updated Christianity without an Incarnation and a Resurrection will not be more successful than similar denials of the past. Shorn of the *supernatural*, and faith in Jesus as God manifest in flesh, the Christian faith is left bare. Accepting such heresies the church can only decline, and men will seek elsewhere for their souls' needs. Describing *The Brook*, Tennyson has the couplet—

> For men may come and men may go,
> But I go on for ever.

Satanically inspired deniers of all the Scriptures teach lies regarding the virgin-born, sinless, and victorious Lord, who triumphed over sin and Satan, death and hell. This unique, wonderful Christ is ever "the same yesterday, and today, and for ever" (Heb. 13:8). Let us, therefore, not be "carried about with many and strange doctrines," even although they emanate from religious sources, but "earnestly contend for the faith which was once delivered unto the saints" (Jude 3).

> Though with a scornful wonder
>   Men see her sore opprest,
> By schisms rent asunder,
>   By heresies distrest;
> Yet saints their watch are keeping,
>   Their cry goes up, "How long?"
> And soon the night of weeping
>   Shall be the morn of song.
>   *Author Unknown*

2. Modern Divisions

Satan has ever been the destroyer of unity. He ruined it among the angels, hence his fall and the casting out of those who took his side. He severed the harmony between God and man, hence the fall of Adam. He blasted the communion existing between man and man, hence the slaughter of Abel by Cain.

The disintegration within the church, from the time of its inception, had its birth in Satan's evil heart. He has ever been conscious of the fact that the mystical union binding believers to the Lord can never be broken. Mutual communion can be severed as, alas, it is. One has said that God made the church; man made denominations. But we would like to know how far man was inspired by Satan in such creations. What schisms, bitter feuds, estrangements, splits, and divisions we have, all in the name of denomination or undenominationalism.

We maintain that the present tragic disintegration of Christian forces is Satan's masterpiece in these last days to destroy the witness and testimony the church should have. It is his attack at the church's head. Being the Lord's creation "by water and by blood" and destined to function as his representative in the world, the church has ever been hated by the devil. If, therefore, he can succeed in getting her members to fight against each other instead of fighting together against a common foe, he then succeeds in limiting the application of our Lord's redemptive work to a lost world, which work is ever destructive to Satan's power and dominion. Alas, Christians ignorant of his devices have allowed him to secure an advantage over them by the divisions in the ranks (1 Cor. 1:10–14; 12:25).

Before leaving this aspect of our study, it will be remembered that the devil has ever preserved unity among his own infernal hosts. Splits, divisions, and rebellions never seem to divide his flock. The diabolical foes of Christ and his church swear constant allegiance to their prince and are one in the covenant of destruction of all that is spiritual. Satan never casts out Satan! The church, however, ravaged by his attacks upon her, is torn asunder by schisms, and consequently she is destitute of authority in the world. May the prayer of her glorious head be speedily answered: "That they may be one!"

3. Modern Unbelief

Modernism is guilty of *disbelief*. Unbelief, or *nonbelief*, however, is characteristic of a godless world. To those who are lost in their sin, the gospel is hid or veiled. Satan, the god of this world, has "blinded the minds of them which believe not" (2 Cor. 4:3,4). He resorts to all kinds of means to keep the souls of men in total darkness regarding the true nature of the glorious gospel of Christ.

The number of those who sit in darkness is colossal. One is well-nigh cast down in despair as they think of the millions Satan is robbing of the Savior. We have lived to see the day of tremendous apathy regarding spiritual things. So-called Christian lands are becoming more pagan with the passing days. There is a great sweep of anti-religious forces the world over. Worldliness has swamped our homes and religious life. Clear-cut Christian work was never so hard as it is in this carnal-minded age. Blindly the multitudes are rushing on to a lost eternity. Drunk with the wine of pleasure, they fail to realize what a rude awakening will be theirs when, in hell with a grinning devil standing over them to mock at their moans, they will realize all too late that the door of mercy is fast closed. Oh, that man could come to learn the cruel heartlessness of Satan as he strives to rob Christ of souls, and souls of Christ. May ours be the Spirit-empowered ministry of arousing men and women to the devices of Satan!

4. Modern Destructions

It would seem as if Satan is a Mr. Facing-Both-Ways in this age. He has a sort of Dr. Jekyll and Mr. Hyde existence. The "angel of light" is the mask covering this face as the "roaring lion." But no matter how angelic he may appear to be, through all his activities one increasing purpose is in his heart. Murder is there! A murderer from the beginning, he has ever remained a monster of destruction and death.

Now, these are days of increased gospel activity, both at home and abroad. Think of the way in which radio, television, and Christian literature are helping to bring the gospel to millions! But with such, there is increased satanic activity. Urged on by his own murderous heart, the devil is out to destroy as many as he can before they have a chance of turning to the Savior.

Conscious of his own final doom, conscious that there is no salvation whatever for him, Satan is working with feverish haste to crowd the caverns of the doomed. Truly his sickle of death is never idle! Think of World War II, with the millions slain, and of the wars since that dark period! Think of the bloody revolutions within the last twenty years! Think of the thousands who are being killed every year upon the streets of our land!

Let us make no mistake about it: we, too, will be open to his murderous attacks if, resisting him, we yet dare to stand out and confess to a devil-driven world that there is deliverance from Satan's cruel bondage. If we are Spirit-filled, the emissaries of hell will contrive to shorten our days; but we are ever safe in Christ's hand, for no satanic shaft can strike till the Son of God sees fit. Hallelujah!

AFTER THE CHURCH PERIOD

We have now reached a further and final stage in the bitter antagonism between the archenemy of God and man.

With superb generalship, Satan is to marshal his hordes together for a decisive conflict. In fact, John reminds us in the Book of Revelation, recording as it does the human and hellish factors in this titanic struggle, that knowing his time is short, the devil is to manifest great wrath. Woe be to the inhabitants of earth when the devil and his hosts are loose among them!

Having failed to annihilate "the Seed" in the Old Testament, and to destroy Christ in his day, and to prevail against the true church in her age, Satan now concentrates his attention upon the multitudes left behind at the translation of the church.

With the removal of the church, the earth will witness the culmination of antichristian forces controlled by "the Antichrist." This ape of God, personally inspired and indwelt by Satan, the Antichrist of all antichrists, will be a terror to all those living during the Tribulation period.

Perhaps the devil's greatest work at the commencement of this period will be the denial of the miracle of the church's translation, and the beguiling of souls through counterfeit miracles. He will do his utmost to thwart the influences of our resurrection even as he labored to nullify the power of Christ's resurrection.

A display of God's power has ever called forth the wrath of the devil. The miraculous birth of Christ was answered by the murder of the innocents by Herod; the benediction of the Father at Jordan was met by the fierce temptation of the wilderness; the coming of the Spirit at Pentecost was the occasion of extreme persecution. Outbursts of revival in the church's history have ever been followed by greater activity on the part of Satan. With the glorious miracle of the church's translation at hand, all hell is moved to counteract the influence of such a stupendous display of God's power and grace.

DURING THE TRIBULATION

The concluding Book of the Bible was rightly placed in such a divine library. It records the consummation of all things, even of the devil and his works, hence his hatred of "The Revelation," and his subtlety in keeping people from studying it.

What a Book of conflicts it is! It carries the clash of arms all through its pages. Within it the stage is set for the greatest drama of all ages. Tearing off all disguises, Satan is open and avowed in his antagonism and prepared for a spectacular overthrow of Christ and his anointed.

Briefly, then, let us trace the climax of the conflict of the ages, which we have been trying to depict in these pages.

For the first half of the Tribulation, Satan tries to win the kingdom by flatteries. He comes in peaceably and religiously, as he can when occasion demands it. He inspires his agent to set himself up in the place of God as *GOD*. Gradually, however, his real nature is revealed, and he stands out as the enemy of the Lord, and of his ancient people, the Jews.

Two avenues of Satan's hate and power are before us in this tragic period: namely, the reign of the Antichrist, who represents a vast, apostate civil and political power; and the ministry of the False Prophet, who functions as the head of religious apostasy. So Christ's right to govern the world is challenged by the Antichrist; and Christ's right to the worship of his own is challenged by the False Prophet.

At the end of this period, however, Christ descends to earth and, routing his foes, both demonic and human, takes unto himself his power and reigns. The description given of the carnage produced by such a conflict is indeed terrible and should lead us to praise God anew that we shall be away from the earth when it transpires.

AFTER THE TRIBULATION

We frankly admit that the Book of Revelation contains symbolic language difficult to understand. Still, it was meant to be read, and a special blessing is pronounced and promised to those who study the book. Neglect of it, however, is general among Christians, and such negligence is produced by the devil, since the book records his own doom.

With the setting up of his kingdom, Christ commits Satan to the bottomless pit for a thousand years. What a relief for a sin-cursed, war-scarred world! Think of it! The earth without a devil! Christ is in supreme control, and reigns from shore to shore. For a millennium he has undisputed sway, "where'er the sun doth its successive journeys run."

As to the devil, he cannot manifest his antagonism, since he is in prison and has no power to emerge out of his sealed abyss. What irony there is in the phrase "set a seal upon him"! Upon the prison of Christ's sepulchre a seal was set declaring that he would not rise, but "He tore the bars away, Jesus, my Lord." Satan's abode is sealed, but he had no power to rise. He is detained, for One greater than he has prevailed, and has sent him to the abyss.

Personal Activity for a Little Season

At the end of the thousand years, Satan is allowed to leave his prison and, by his deception of the nations, proves that even a millenium in which to reflect and repent works no change in his diabolical nature. The stored-up rage of a thousand years is vomited out upon Christ and the multitudes he reigned over in peace and righteousness. Gathering the deceived nations together, Satan enters his final conflict. What a blessing it will be that Satan is only to be loosed for "a little season"! But released he is, to show that he is still a devil.

One may wonder why so many of earth's people follow Satan, after the glorious benefits of Christ's personal reign. With all the peace and felicity of such a kingdom, surely Satan will have to fight his concluding battle alone. It must not be forgotten, however, that multitudes only yield feigned obedience to Christ during the Millennium. Although Satan is imprisoned in the bottomless pit, the satanic spirit is still imprisoned in many hearts and finds expression as soon as their cruel master is released.

We have no account of the demons being cast into prison along with their prince. During the Millennium, many of them are at large, and doubtless are active in the minds of thousands. Open hostility, however, is impossible, owing to Christ's complete control of all things.

Personal Subjectivity Forever

With the setting up of the Great White Throne, we reach the final subjugation of Satan. The mills of God may grind slowly but they grind exceeding sure. Christ, the Seed of the woman, whom Satan tried to destroy, was manifested that he might destroy the works of the devil. At Calvary he was virtually deposed, and now, gathering together the fruits of redemptive work, Christ disposes once and for all of his satanic foe. The devil is cast into the lake of fire and brimstone, there to be tormented day and night forever and ever.

What an end for an angelic being once having high rank in the courts of heaven! Behold, how the mighty are fallen! The history of this Lucifer can be briefly traced. Once in heaven, he was deposed and cast out into the air. From the air he comes to earth. Then comes the bottomless pit, and after such, the earth again, which in turn is followed by his sojourn in the lake of fire and brimstone forever and ever.

At last Christ is absolutely supreme. All enemies are under his feet. Satan and sin are finally banished and a new creation is presented to the Father, who becomes all in all.

> Evil at last shall fall,
> Christ shall gain the victory,
> And God shall be all in all.

The earth and heaven, we are told, flee away from Christ as he sits upon his august throne. *Why the earth?* Because for millenniums it was cursed by sin and came to bear the stain of the Redeemer's blood. So a new earth is provided, into which Satan, sin, sorrow, and separation can never enter. *Why the heavens?* Because they had been polluted by Satan's presence as the prince of the power of the air. Such heavenly spheres could never be clean in the Lord's sight. Thus they give place to heavens as pure as the One creating them.

The conclusion of the whole matter which we have been considering is that we must understand how to use our weapons of warfare, so that as we tarry amid the shadows of a satanically controlled world, we may be more than conquerors.

It would be blessed, indeed, if God took us immediately to his heavenly house, but he never does. He leaves us in a world filled with temptation and sin: "From every bush the lances start." We have to move through the heart of the enemy's country, and a thousand solicitations from within and without would have us yield to the foe.

The weapons of the world are of no avail in such a conflict with the powers of darkness. We must have more divine, more spiritual, more celestial aids. And we have them in him who is our Jehovah Nissi—the Lord of Hosts our Banner. He has made every provision for us to be delivered from the pomp and power of the enemy, from the subtle craft and poisonous sweetness of the tempter.

The Weapons of the Word

The Word of God, Paul reminds us, is the Sword of the Spirit, and a very effective sword it is when wielded against Satan. It was with this weapon that our Lord defeated the enemy as he tempted him in the wilderness. If we are to be victorious as we wield the Spirit's Sword, we must have more than a mere intelligent conception of the contents of the Bible. Ours must be a living experience of its power.

One reason Satan has tried to destroy faith and confidence in the Bible as the inspired Word of God is that he knows only too well its effectiveness as a weapon when used against him.

The Weapon of the Blood

As the accuser, the devil can be overcome by the blood of the Lamb. In hours of temptation, the blood ever avails as we plead its efficacy. Satan is a defeated foe, and such a defeat can be actualized in our lives as we seek the shelter of the blood. May we learn how to bring the work of the cross to bear upon all the wiles and machinations of the enemy. "They overcame him by the blood of the Lamb" (Rev. 12:11).

The Weapon of Resistance

Scripture affirms that if we resist the devil, he will flee from us. We have the prerogative of saying, with the Master, "Get thee behind me, Satan!" Because he is neither omnipotent, omnipresent, omniscient, or sovereign, we can overcome him as we resist him in the victory of our omnipotent, omnipresent, omniscient, sovereign Lord.

Had our Lord been merely man, he could not have had power over the devil and demons, but being the Son of God with power, he could exercise authority even in the infernal regions. It is this power which, in virtue of his cross, resurrection, ascension, and gift of the Holy Spirit, he shares with his believing people. May ours be the grace of appropriation!

The Weapon of Vigilance

We are exhorted to watch and pray lest we enter into temptation. To watch and pray means to have one eye on the devil and the other on the Lord for deliverance.

> Principalities and powers
>   Mustering their unseen array,
> Wait for thy unguarded hour;
>   Watch and pray.
> > *Author Unknown*

A legend tells of a high and mighty conclave Satan held in hell to receive the reports of his evil angels' work. After a while, one of the fiendish assembly arose and said, "I saw a caravan of Christians crossing the desert, and I raised a terrible simoom and destroyed them all." "What of that?" responded Satan. "Their souls were saved."

Another demon rose to say, "I saw a ship conveying missionaries and their band of workers to another clime, and I let loose upon them the winds of heaven, and they sank into a watery grave." "What of that?" replied the tempter. "Their souls were all saved."

There was a moment's pause in that ghastly company, and then another demonic spirit arose and hissed, "I tried for seven years to send a Christian to sleep; and at last I succeeded." "You have done well," returned the devil, and the vaults of the abyss rang with plaudits and fiendish laughter.

Beloved, it is no fiction that Satan laughs when Christians sleep. Lulled to sleep on the lap of some Delilah, a Christian will work more harm than a thousand worldlings. Prayerless and careless, we aid the devil in his work of deceit and destruction. Let us not sleep as do others, but let us watch and be sober.

Vigilant we must be, seeing that the devourer is abroad destroying souls. We must awake the sinner, lest he sleep the sleep which knows no waking, till the trump of doom arouses him. Opportunities are becoming fewer, and before long the season of service will be over. *Mox Nox*, says the dial at Abbortsford—*The Night Cometh*. Let us, therefore, be alert. Let us talk together as did *Christian* and *Hopeful* upon *Enchanted Ground*. Let us keep one another awake to the prospects of glory, awake to the devices of Satan, awake to the need of a perishing world, awake to the responsibilities of our calling, until at length we reach the *Celestial city*, where we shall work without wearying and rest without reclining.

> Sleep is for sons of night—
> Ye are children of the light,
> Yours is the glory bright;
> Wake, Brethren! Wake!

Author Unknown

The Weapon of Faith

"This is the victory that overcometh the world, even our faith" (1 John 5:4). Of course, there is no virtue in faith itself. The virtue is in the One to whom faith links us. Having the Son of God, the promises of God, the Spirit of God, let us possess our possessions and use them against our common foe.

No room has been left for devil-defeated lives in the divine program. Our weapons are mighty, even to the pulling down of satanic strongholds, but we must appropriate these all-powerful weapons by faith, and use them against the enemy. When we are strong in faith, then we know what it is to be a terror to the devil. Oh, to be feared by Satan! Oh, to live in God, and by faith, so that he will cringe before our Spirit-inspired life and witness! Let us not forget that it is written, ". . . one shall chase a thousand, and two put [not two but] ten thousand to flight." No matter in what form we may have to meet the

undying antagonism of Satan, may ours be the paean of
triumph—"Thanks be unto God who giveth us the victory!"

> To Thee, and to Thy Christ, O God,
>   We sing, we ever sing;
> For He the lonely winepress trod
>   Our cup of joy to bring.
> His glorious arm the strife maintained,
>   He marched in might from far;
> His robes were with the vintage stained,
>   Red with the wine of war.
>
> To Thee, and to Thy Christ, O God,
>   We sing, we ever sing.
> For He invaded Death's abode
>   And robbed him of his sting.
> The abuse of dust enthralls no more,
>   For He, the Strong to save,
> Himself doth guard that silent door,
>   Great Keeper of the grave.
>
> To Thee, and to Thy Christ, O God,
>   We sing, we ever sing;
> For He hath crushed beneath His rod
>   The world's proud rebel king.
> He plunged in His imperial strength
>   To gulfs of darkness down,
> He brought His trophy up at length,
>   The foiled usurper's crown.
>
> To Thee, and to Thy Christ, O God,
>   We sing, we ever sing;
> For He redeemed us with His blood
>   From every evil thing.
> Thy saving strength His Arm upbore,
>   The Arm that set us free;
> Glory, O God, for evermore,
>   Be to Thy Christ and Thee.
>
> *—Mrs. Cousin*

For this purpose the Son of God was manifested, that he might destroy the works of the devil (1 John 3:8).

Satan the Defeated Foe

In many ways, the First Epistle of John is one of the most remarkable letters in the New Testament. It is a precious pearl of divine revelation, particularly in connection with Satan and his nature and works. It is a family letter from the father to his little children who are in the world surrounded by evil forces. Sin in the believer is treated as a child's offense against his father and is dealt with as a family matter (2:1).

The Epistle is full of sharp contrasts, which even a casual reading makes clear—Christ and Antichrist; God and the devil; light and darkness; life and death; holiness and sin; love and hate; the truthful and the liars; the overcomers and the defeated; the Savior, who is the leader of the good, and Satan, who is the monarch of all who are evil. The Epistle is, therefore, a gallery of battles, and represents the greatest of all conflicts in history, namely, the never-ending war between good and evil. The comforting and inspiring message for the heart of God's children is that "greater is he that is in you, than he that is in the world"— *he that is in you,* referring to our all-conquering God; *he that is in the world,* meaning Satan, the unceasing antagonist of God and man (4:4).

1. The Sinister Greatness of Satan

The Bible never attempts to dispute or deny the greatness of Satan's wisdom and might. In the previous chapters of this study we endeavored to prove that he was created the highest of all angelic beings when *"all* the angels [of God] shouted for joy"* (Job 38:7, TLB). As an archangel he possessed a marvelous intellect, unique and perfect knowledge, but through pride his original greatness was perverted and since his Fall, his power has been used to blast rather than bless. His great hold on humanity may be attributed to the fact that he has assailed every soul since Eve. Satan preferred, as John Milton puts it, to—

> Reign in Hell than serve in Heaven
>   And with ambitious aim
> Against the Throne and Monarchy of God,
> Raised impious war in Heaven.

But although he continues his impious war, with his legions of darkness, the devil is a defeated foe. One greater than he appeared and by his life, death and resurrection robbed him of his power and authority, and destroyed his works. Fight on, he may, but he knows only too well that One greater than he is in the world to liberate those in his cruel bondage.

> What though in the conflict for right
>   Your enemies almost prevail!
> God's armies just hid from sight
>   Are more than the foes which assail.
>   *Author Unknown*

2. THE SUPERIOR GREATNESS OF THE SAVIOR

How the saints John wrote to must have been heartened by his inspired declarations regarding the conquest of Satan by Christ! They lived in days permeated with the spirit of antichrist, and overcame the influence of false teachers by the faith that the Jesus indwelling them was far greater than the god of this world. Being begotten of God the wicked one could not seduce them (1 John 5:18). The supreme purpose of the Incarnation was the destruction of the works of the devil (1 John 3:8). This superior greatness of Jesus is based upon the fact that although Satan has power, he is not all powerful as Jesus is because he is—

The Omnipotent Lord

Satan may possess potent forces united in their diabolical purpose, for Satan never casts out Satan, but he does not share the omnipotence of deity. Christ met his adversary alone, and singlehandedly assailed the host of wickedness and triumphed gloriously over them. Had he wished, he could have summoned a host of unfallen angels to assist, but, like David of old, he preferred to meet his Goliath alone and, thereby, make his disaster and defeat more overwhelming. The strong man has been bound by the One who has the preeminence, and is Lord of all.

> Jesus is stronger than Satan or sin,
>   Satan to Jesus must bow;
> Therefore I triumph without and within,
>   Jesus saves me now.

The Omniscient Lord

He is not only all-powerful, but also all-wise, all-knowing, all-intelligent. Great wisdom was certainly bestowed upon Satan, when he was created as Lucifer, but he was not given omniscience, which is the prerogative of deity alone. He can understand the subtleties of the human heart and reach it by choosing from a thousand forms of temptation he has developed through many millenniums, but Christ is far wiser in that he can discern satanic approaches afar off. He can read the devil's mind, but the devil cannot read his mind. This is clear from our Lord's warning to Peter, "Satan hath desired to have you, that he may sift you as wheat" (Luke 22:31). Able, then, to discern his evil intentions, Christ is likewise able to circumvent them.

The Omnipresent Lord

Omnipresence is another quality deity alone possesses, and man can never flee from God's presence, even if he goes to the uttermost parts of the sea (Ps. 139). As the result of his resurrection, and the advent of the Holy Spirit, Jesus promised his own that he would be with them always, no matter where they were in the world (Matt. 28:20). But Satan cannot be everywhere at the same time, as his Conqueror can. We concede that he has universal influence, for the whole world is in the lap of such a wicked one, but his actual presence, like his power, is limited. It is common for us to say that certain persons are doing certain things when actually their agents are acting on their behalf and in their name and authority. A commanding general cannot be on every part of the battlefield at the same time, but his officers under him execute his orders and carry out his commands. Likewise, an ambassador represents the head of his country and speaks and acts on his behalf.

This is so with Satan, who is not able to work in all hearts at the same time. Yet, through all the evil subordinates under his control and mastery, he can fulfil his base designs. Thoroughly imbibed with his spirit, roaming hordes of demons act as he would. He is in contact with all "his angels," having a sort of spiritual radio by which he can communicate orders and receive reports. How we bless the Lord, for his omnipresence, enabling him to promise that no matter where we may go in the world he will never leave nor forsake us!

The Sinless Lord

The testimony of John in his matchless Epistle is that Jesus is the personification of unblemished holiness. He is light and in him is no darkness at all. But Satan is likened to the darkness, which is not positively powerful in the light. Darkness is the absence of light—a negation. Light is not the absence of darkness only, but something real and positive. Darkness in your room was the absence of the sun before it arose. Darkness cannot affect the sunlight, but such light banishes darkness.

Christ is portrayed as infinite holiness, and, as the Light of the World, he can positively banish all darkness. Because of his perfection, he can dispel all evil and satanic influences, and ultimately will disperse them, for in glory, there is "no night there."

> He comes, from thickest films of vice
> To clear the mental ray,
> And on the eye-balls of the blind
> To pour celestial day.

Likewise, in his Christ-glorifying gospel, John assures us of his Master's holiness and consequent victory over the evil one. His is the gospel of triumph! The apostle records that Jesus used the designation of Satan, "The prince of this world," twice over, but with a different association in each case. First of all, Jesus assured his disciples that "Now is the judgment of this world: now shall the prince of this world be cast out" (John 12:31). Weymouth translates it, "Now comes judgement upon this world: now will the Prince of this world be driven out."

The Greek word for "judgment" used here means *crisis*,

and refers to something to be accomplished by his death.
The judgment of all mankind is still in the future.
Anticipating his death by crucifixion, Jesus declares a
victory over Satan's domain, with divine exultation and
triumph. Calvary was to mean the emancipation of souls
from satanic bondage—the *crisis*, when provision would
be secured from sin's defilement and dominion. As Barnes
expresses it in his monumental *Notes on the New Testament:*

> "Now is approaching the decisive scene, the eventful
> period—*the crisis*—when it shall be determined who shall
> rule the world. There has been a long conflict between the
> powers of light and darkness—between God and the Devil.
> Satan has so far effectually ruled, that he may be said to be
> the prince of this world. But my approaching death will
> destroy his kingdom; will break down his power; and will be
> the means of setting up the kingdom of God over man." The
> death of Christ was to be the most grand and effectual of all
> means that could be used to establish the authority of the
> law and the government of God, Rom 8:3,4. . . . The death
> of Jesus was the determining cause, the grand crisis, the
> concentration of all that God had ever done, or will ever do,
> to break down the kingdom of Satan, and set up His power
> over man. . . . It was the fulfillment of the prediction of
> Genesis 3:15.

The second reference to "the prince of darkness" is
connected with our Lord's assertion of his sinlessness.
"The prince of this world cometh, and hath nothing in me"
(John 14:30). As the prince and head of the rulers of this
dark world, Satan has had power over the masses under his
control and subject to his will. Jesus, however, was never
under his influence or captivated by his seductive approach. "In me, Satan has nothing to appeal to, nothing at
all." There was no guilt in him to give authority to the
enemy's terrors, no corruption within his heart to give the
tempter advantage in his temptations. Jesus was destitute
of any principle or feeling in sympathy with Satan's desires

and designs. Where there is no such principle, temptation has no power, hence the victory of Jesus when tempted by him. By his death, he would make it possible for Satan to be cast out of sin-bound lives, but with him there was no need of such an expulsion, seeing the prince of the world never had a foothold in his being (Col. 2:14,15).

Jesus was born holy and undefiled. The angel said to the Virgin Mary, "The Holy Spirit will come upon you, and the power of the Most High will overshadow you; and for this reason your offspring will be called holy, 'the Son of God'" (Luke 1:35, Weymouth). This is why he is "separate from sinners," all of whom were conceived in sin and "shapen in iniquity (Ps. 51:5)," meaning that because of original sin they are born with evil propensities within. But Jesus was without the old Adamic nature, and therefore, destitute of any evil bias to which Satan could appeal or work upon. With sinners it is different, for they are under the influence of Satan from their birth because of a sinning nature.

Jesus, however, was born with an unsinning nature, and thus appealed to the knowledge his accusers had of his sinless life: "Which of you convicts me of sin?" (John 8:46, Weymouth). He also reminded them of his entire conformity to his Father's will: "I do always those things that please [my Father]" (John 8:29). He was thus distinct from all others, for never had he cast a shadow on the brightness of the vision of his father's presence by the least sympathy with evil. Through all his thirty-three years, Jesus remained as pure as God in heaven, passing through a world of sin and satanic allurements as a sunbeam through a hovel without a stain.

There was no territory in his being to which Satan could lay claim, nothing in him that had affinity with sin. Thus, his appeal was one that "spotless purity alone could make, and in his own testimony uttered in the dignity of certain knowledge." When he said to his disciples, "the prince of this world is coming," the reference was to the effort of Satan to try him in the dreadful conflict and agency of Gethsemane and Calvary. But He faced the powers of darkness, and, as the thrice Holy One, triumphed gloriously over them.

Sinners are born with one nature, namely, one prone to evil; and Jesus was born with one nature, namely, an unsinning one. The saints have two natures, namely, the old Adamic nature and the new nature in Christ Jesus. The nature of, and conflict between, these dual natures is fully dealt with by Paul in Romans 7 and 8. "When I would do good, evil is present with me." The conflict of the Holy Spirit with the flesh, the enmity between the carnal mind and the spiritual mind, are constant in the experience of the true child of God. But greater is he who is in us than he who is in the world, and through his finished work of the cross we can live in triumph (2 Cor. 2:14).

> The gates of brass before Him burst,
> The iron fetters yield.

We are doomed to failure if we try to meet Satan on his own ground. Our only hope of victory is to meet him in the virtue and power of the Redeemer. There is a story of a swan wobbling along the shore of a lake, when a hungry wolf appeared and would have torn the swan to pieces. But the swan said to itself, "If I am not strong on land, I am strong in the water," so in it plunged and the wolf followed. The swan turned around and with its strong bill gripped the ear of the wolf and dragged its head under the water and held it there until the beast was drowned. The point is clear. If we assail the satanic wolf in our own strength and on its ground, we are bound to lose in the conflict. It is only as we meet the wolf on the Lord's ground, and drag it to the fountain filled with blood drawn from his veins, that we experience what it is to be more than conquerors (Rev. 12:10,11).

It is to be feared that many of us, who claim to be the Lord's, are not as fully aware as we should be of the corruption, and therefore the danger, of the sinning nature we inherited, and for which we become responsible when we reach the age of accountability. The hymn reminds us that—

> They who fain would serve Thee best,
> *Are* conscious most of wrong within.

It was only when Isaiah had a vision of the august holiness of the Lord, and saw him as the King, the Lord of hosts, that he came to cry, "Woe is me! for I am undone; because I am a man of unclean lips, and I dwell in the midst of a people of unclean lips" (6:1–8). But we need not fear the white light of divine holiness, for what the light reveals, the blood can cleanse. With live coals from off the altar, sin is purged. These are days when Satan is at war with the saints, and the onslaught becomes fiercer with the passing days. But if the thirst for holiness is ours, then appropriating the triumph of Calvary we can successfully resist the devil. The God of peace is able to bruise Satan under our feet (Rom. 16:20). "To bruise" means to subdue, to gain a victory over, and this is what God makes real in our experience over the wiles of the devil, as we abide beneath our heavenly Father's shadow.

The holiest among us need victory, in some form or another, and to discover more fully the secret of overcoming power. It was while the psalmist was in the presence of God within his sanctuary that he realized what he was actually like in God's sight: "So foolish was I, and ignorant: I was as a beast before thee" (73:22). See Job 30:29. Some form of animal also led others to discover a particular form of vice of which they were guilty. "Man is like the beasts that perish" (Ps. 49:12,20). Solomon wrote, "I said in mine heart concerning . . . the sons of men, that God might

manifest them, and that they might see that they themselves are beasts" (Eccl. 3:18). Peter has some strong
language regarding those who act like "natural brute
beasts" (2 Peter 2:12)—a figure of speech Jude also uses
(Jude 10). Man is able to tame every kind of beast, but has
a tyrant of a tongue he finds it very difficult to harness
(James 3:7).

Scripture often refers to man as being *Brutish:* "Every
man is brutish" (Jer. 10:8,14; 51:17). Even *pastors* became
"brutish" (10:21). See Proverbs 30:2. We have only to
think of the vandalism, violence, raping of women, murderous attacks on defenseless people, so characteristic of
human society today, to see how brutish or bestial men can
be. It is interesting how various animals represent some
aspect of the sin of which man is guilty. In the Bible *Zoo*
we have mention of a large number of animals, as if to
show how man in his depravity, corruption, sensuality and
indifference to holy things can become. James wrote of
those who were "earthly, sensual, devilish" (3:15). Here
are the different forms of animal life referred to in
Scripture, along with their reputed characteristics:

THE ASS (Prov. 26:3)—*stupid, indolent.*
THE BEAR (Dan. 7:5), also the SLOTH, of India and Ceylon
—*rough, fierce, surly, sluggish, lazy.*
THE BOAR (Ps. 80:13)—*cruel, coarse.*
THE BULLOCK (Jer. 31:18)—*uncontrollably strong.*
THE DOG (Prov. 26:17; Matt. 7:6; Phil. 3:2; 2 Peter 2:22)—
greedy, wild, malevolent, contemptible.
THE DRAGON (Job 30:29)—*fearsome, loves darkness.*
THE FOX (Song of Sol. 2:15; Matt. 8:20; Luke 13:32)—
cunning, fraudulent, destructive.
THE GOAT (Matt. 25:32)—*unyielding, oppressive.*
THE HORSE (Ps. 32:9)—*impatient of control, destructive.*
THE HORSELEECH (Prov. 30:15)—*greedy, selfish.*
THE LEOPARD, or PANTHER (Jer. 13:23; Rev. 13:2)—
deceptive, treacherous, wrathful.
THE LION (2 Tim. 4:17)—*ferocious, angry, arbitrarily uses
power.*

THE MULE (Ps. 32:9)—*stubborn, insensitive.*
THE OX (Isa. 1:3)—*obstinate, brutal.*
THE PEACOCK (Job 39:13)—*proud, self-important.*
THE SERPENT (Matt. 10:16)—*subtle, stealthy, treacherous.*
THE SWINE (Matt. 7:6; 2 Peter 2:22)—*unclean in nature and practice.*
THE VULTURE or EAGLE (Matt. 24:28; Job 28:7)—*keen vision for purpose of destruction.*
THE VIPER (Matt. 23:33)—*venomous, slanderous, poisonous.*
THE WOLF (Matt. 7:15; Acts 20:29)—*violent, rapacious.*

Satan's last embodiments will be "a beast rising up out of the sea" and "another beast coming up out of the earth" (Rev. 13:1,11). The three animals identified with them—the leopard, bear and lion—are given by Daniel as "symbols of the empires that preceded Rome, and whose characteristics all entered into the qualities of the Roman Empire: Macedonian, *swiftness of conquest*, Persian, *tenacity of purpose*, Babylonish, *voracity*, Dan. 7:4–6."

We can understand Job's feelings when he confessed, "I am a brother to dragons, and a companion to owls" (30:29). Our Adamic, depraved nature is a cage of unclean birds and beasts, and the longer we live and holier we become the more we discover what a menagerie the old nature is with desires and passions that need to be tamed and subdued. Thinking of the beasts of earth we can see the vices cursing humanity embodied in hateful, ugly and repulsive forms. Associated with original sin is something of the cunning of the fox, the treachery of the panther, the revenge of the tiger, and the lust of the swine.

A friend once asked an aged saint what caused him so often to complain of pain and weariness at eventide. "Alas!" he replied, "I have every day so much to do. I have two falcons to tame, two hares to keep from running away, two hawks to manage, a serpent to confine, a lion to chain, and a sick man to tend and wait upon." The friend said to the old man, "You must be joking. Surely no man can have all these things to do at once?" He replied, "Indeed, I am not joking. What I told you is the sad, sober truth; for the two falcons are my two eyes, which I must diligently guard; the two hares are my feet, which want to run in the way of sin; the two hawks are my two hands which I must train to work and provide myself and my brethren in need; the serpent is my tongue I must bridle lest I speak unnecessarily; the lion is my heart with which I continually fight lest evil things come out of it; the sick man is my whole body always needing watchfulness and care. All this wears out my daily strength!"

John could write to those who had overcome the wicked one (1 John 2:13). What is our hope, our secret in overcoming an evil heart, a sinful world and a cruel foe? When the heart rises up like a fox we must allow Jesus who knew how to deal with foxy Herod, to defeat and destroy its cunning. When we feel guilty of deception, we can bring the tendency to the Lion of Judah for he alone can deal with that old serpent, the devil. When lusts arise, we must drag the swine to the blood and choke them all. Let us not fear to meet Satan or sin, no matter in what form they may approach, beautiful or bestial. We have the blessed promise that the Lord is able and willing to deliver us from every evil work, and preserve us unto his heavenly kingdom (2 Tim. 4:18). Let us claim the strength of our Omnipotent Lord and rest in him, confident that he will vanquish the foe seeking to ensnare us. Before long we shall be saved to sin no more.

Robert M. M'Cheyne would have us sing—

> When I stand before the throne
> Dressed in beauty not my own,
> When I see Thee as Thou art,
> Love Thee with unsinning heart;
> Then, Lord, shall I fully know—
> Not till then—how much I owe.

How true !!! Praise God

We have to struggle . . . with . . . the spirit-forces of evil in the heavenly sphere (Eph. 6:12, MOFFATT).

Satan and the Spirit-forces of Evil

It is common knowledge that every part of Scripture has its own distinctive imagery, acting as the medium through which spiritual instruction is conveyed to our hearts. For instance, Amos was a herdsman of Tekoa, and his rich prophecy abounds with illustrations taken from the wild and pastoral region in which he was born and brought up. So we read of the fat kine of Bashan, of lions in the forest, of grasshoppers, of baskets of fruit, of stars, and of other natural objects. David, and David's Greater Son, our Lord Jesus, were both adept at—

"Finding tongues in trees, books in running brooks, Sermons in stones, and good in everything"—

as Shakespeare expresses it in *As You Like It*.

New Testament writers also knew how to ransack every sphere for fitting metaphors or symbols of truth. Paul, in particular, is prominent in his use of figures of speech to enforce his message. It would be profitable to gather together all the types of illustrations he used in the

99

peerless Epistles he wrote. It would seem as if he ransacked all aspects and relationships of life as media of expression.

As a close observer of the might and grandeur of Rome's legions, we can understand the apostle's use of military metaphors to proclaim the manifold truths of the gospel. Rome was then the mistress of the world, and Paul spent a good deal of his life under the shadow of the greatest military monarchy the world had ever known. He was never far away from soldiers. They guarded him during his imprisonment, and so he wrote of "the soldier who kept him." Some of his Epistles were written in prison. "Remember my bonds" was his request to his friends. We can almost feel and hear the clank of the chain on his ankles as he wrote of himself as an "Ambassador in bonds." Thus, it was natural for him to use military phraseology to enforce his God-given truths. Because of his intimate association with militarism, it would have been unnatural not to do so.

An outstanding example of such an art is the portion in which Paul portrays the Christian life as a battle against angelic powers of evil, and of the armor all believers should put on as good soldiers of Jesus Christ. In the watchful presence of a fully armed soldier, Paul worked out in beautiful detail the spiritual applications of soldier's actions and armor. Such a portion is given in his prison Epistle to the Ephesians, and because we feel that Moffatt's translation most fully expresses Paul's thought, we cite it, as found in Ephesians 6:10–18,

> Be strong in the Lord and in the strength of his might; put on God's armour, so as to be able to stand against the strategems of the devil. For we have to struggle, not with blood and flesh but with the angelic Rulers, the angelic Authorities, the potentates of the dark present, the spirit-forces of evil in the heavenly sphere. So take God's armour, that you may be able to make a stand upon the evil day and hold your ground by overcoming your foe.

Hold your ground, *tighten the belt of truth about your loins, wear integrity as your coat of mail,* and have your *feet* shod *with the stability of the gospel of peace;* above all, take faith as your shield, to enable you to quench all the fire-tipped darts flung by the evil one, put on *salvation as your helmet,* and take *the Spirit as* your *sword* (that is, *the word of God),* praying at all times in the Spirit, with all manner of prayer and entreaty—be alive to that, attend to it unceasingly, interceding on behalf of all the saints.

THE ARENA

While the RSV and modern versions give us "struggle" for the ASV "wrestle," we feel that the idea of wrestling was in the mind of Paul who, doubtless, had watched those massive, muscular Roman wrestlers, manipulating for a throw, and spiritualized the contest, just as he does with runners, boxers, and other sports (1 Cor. 9:24–27). Further, there is no mixing of metaphors here, for the saints are both *wrestlers* and *soldiers,* both of which imply that the Christian life is not a picnic but a battle, not a flowery bed of ease, but a hard, thorny pathway beset by foes.

Jacob wrestled with a mysterious *man,* who could not have been an ordinary angel, seeing that this wrestler who challenged the patriarch found Jacob to be more than a match, touched the hollow of his thigh and crippled him for life. He also blessed Jacob and changed his name to Israel, meaning, "soldier of God." The believer's wrestle, however, is with evil forces. In wrestling, there is the divestment of all encumbrance, the laying aside of every weight (Heb. 12:1). Military armor would be most out of place for a wrestler to wear. As wrestlers against the wily stratagems of the devil, we must divest ourselves of self-sufficiency, self-effort, and self-dependence. Our whole strength in the combat is in the Lord, and in the power of his might. Wrestling means a personal grapple, a hand-to-hand encounter. Each child of God engages in such in the arena of his own heart and conscience, and also in his own particular sphere of service.

Edmund Burke has the observation, "He that *wrestles* with us strengthens our nerves and sharpens our skill. Our antagonist is our helper." How true this is of each saint as he, or she, wrestles against fallen angelic rulers! Such a combat strengthens faith, and inspires them to rest in the might of their invincible Lord. Thinking again of Jacob, we see how apt is the couplet in *As You Like It*:

So, you have *wrestled* well, and overthrown
More than your enemies.
                                        Wm. Shakespeare

Jacob wrestled well, and gathered more than a victory over his opponent—the one-time cheat and supplanter became a prince having power with God. With us, each wrestle or temptation well-won helps us to win another and makes us stronger in resistance. The plural Paul uses, *"We* wrestle," implies that all born-again believers are in a conflict, maintained in Christ and with divine power and wisdom from a dominating position. Such a conflict commences the moment Satan is dethroned in the heart and the Lord Jesus enters. From then on, there is the fight to reclaim what he once possessed. The deeper our love for Jesus and firmer our desire to be separated from the world, the keener and hotter the contest becomes. If we were sinless, there would be no fight, no ground within us for Satan to hold or lose. Jesus could say, "The prince of this world cometh and hath nothing in me." Alas! in us the enemy has something he can work upon, namely, our old Adamic nature. And so "the fight is on, O Christian soldiers," and will continue until we are called home.

THE ANTAGONISTS

The two phrases to underline in Paul's exhortation to those fighting the good faith are *"Not against . . . But against."* Both the negative and the positive sides of the contest are stressed. In ordinary military warfare it is necessary for soldiers to guard themselves against two faults: namely, underrating the power of the foe on the one hand, and overrating their subtlety and prowess on the other. Our attitude must be that of the two spies Joshua sent out, who thoroughly investigated the potential and position of the land and its people before advancing to a victorious combat.

The Negative: "We have to struggle, not with blood and flesh" (Eph. 6:12, Moffatt).

The order usually followed is that of "blood and flesh" as in "not of blood, nor of the will of the flesh" (John 1:13; see also Heb. 2:14), and here in Ephesians 6:12, as Moffatt does. The reverse, however, is found in Matthew 16:17 and 1 Corinthians 15:50. The thought emphasized is that our wrestling is not against mere visible human power, human nature, or human agency in all their manifest forms, but a truceless war with the unseen spiritual powers of evil themselves. In other places in this Epistle Paul urges believers to oppose heathen practices and convinces them of the necessity of rebuking the outward works of darkness, but here, in the verse before us, his warning is not against wicked men, but against wicked spirits.

It is true that our ostensible and immediate enemies and obstacles are material and visible. We are only too conscious of enemies among men—those who dislike, criticize, hinder, and oppose (unkindly, unlovingly, and sometimes cruelly); of those among our friends who are unsympathetic and unspiritual and who seem to block our pathway to fuller service for the Master. Although innocent hindrances in our spiritual life, they act as Peter did in seeking to prevent Jesus from following his predestined course. Flesh and blood we wrestle against continually in the form of our carnal and corrupt nature. We have to die daily to the works and desires of the flesh, which does not die—we die to it. Human agencies are also prominent in those visible forces operating against deep spirituality, whether political, commercial, social, or religious. All of these tangible foes are but the media of satanic assault.

The Positive: "We have to struggle . . . with the angelic Rulers, the angelic Authorities, the potentates of the dark present, the spirit-forces of evil in the heavenly sphere" (Eph. 6:12, Moffatt). Here Paul bids us to look beyond the secondary causes of hostility to the first cause, namely the devil and his angels, seeing our main controversy is with the invisible spirits of wickedness. Our warfare is against the sources and origin of evil, operating through all persons, circumstances and visible persons for our defeat. We wrestle and fight against the central force of all antagonism to Christ in the spiritual world. Let us examine more closely the diagnosis Paul gives us of the persistent and powerful adversaries, both of Christ and his followers.

1. The Wiles of the Devil (Eph. 6:11)

Moffatt gives us "the stratagems of the devil." The devil is placed first for he is the great arch-foe, the mastermind behind all evil figures and forces. The term "wiles" used here is also found in chapter 4:14, in the phrase "the sleight of men, and cunning craftiness, whereby they lie in wait to deceive." The devil has the craftiness, the stratagems of a skilful manipulator devoted to the systematic plan of deceit—a methodical subtlety perfected through millennia of operation. His arts, cunning devices, and snares to drag souls down to his own prescribed perdition are innumerable.

Paul would have us remember that the devil does not meet the Christian soldier face to face. Open warfare is not among his tactics. He makes his approach in darkness and employs the method of cunning rather than power—

deludes rather than vanquishes by mere force. Like a snake in the grass, he insidiously attacks. His pattern of warfare is by ambushes and surprises. This is why the soldier must be constantly armed. It is easier to encounter an open foe than a hidden, sly and stealthy one. And the devil is the wise controlling force behind and directing all his evil hosts against the Christian.

He approaches and assaults us whether directly or indirectly not in "repulsive forms, but comes to recommend some plausible doctrine to lay before us some temptation that shall not immediately repel us," comments Barnes. "He presents the world in an alluring aspect; invites to pleasures that seem to be harmless; and leads us in indulgence, until we have gone so far that we cannot retreat."

We do not recognize as we should the fearful ranks of evil powers, represented by the satanic foes of the hosts of the Lord. Perfectly mobilized, organized by the subtle fiends of hell, these dark spirits are in conflict with the bodies and souls of men who, unless they are completely covered by the whole armor of God, have no might against such dread foes. Paul goes on to describe the formidable forces of order and strength of these unseen, evil powers.

2. Angelic Rulers (Eph. 6:12)

These are the "principalities" among evil spirits with delegated authority, "the despotisms," as Weymouth translates the term. What must be borne in mind is the fact that the angelic hierarchy with its succession of different orders of superhuman power is used of invisible forces both good and evil. (See Rom. 8:38; Eph. 1:21; 3:10; Col. 1:16.) In the portion before us Paul uses the terms to describe evil powers, with their appointed sphere of government, and the authority which is committed to it. The fallen angels under Satan's control are despots, invested with tyrannical power, leaders of a vast organized spiritual world dedicated to the destruction of all that is holy.

3. Angelic Authorities (Eph. 6:12)

If *ruler* relates to dignity of position, *authorities*, or chieftains, suggests power to act. *Might and dominion* are terms suggesting natural force and the moral force of dignity or lordship, in which it is clothed. In *Paradise Lost*, Milton represents Satan as addressing the fallen angels as "Thrones, Dominions, Princedoms, Virtues, and Powers." The glorious hope is that our blessed Lord will "put down all rule, and all authority and power" (1 Cor. 15:24). Even now, with all their position and power, the satanic hierarchy is like a dog on a leash, and cannot go any further than divine permission, as the trial of Job portrays.

4. The Potentates of the Dark Present (Eph. 6:12)

The KJV translation of the phrase, "the rulers of the darkness of this world," is akin to Moffatt's—"the forces that control and govern this dark world." Satan, as the god of this world, loves darkness rather than light, and he has appointed some of his evil servants as the rulers of such darkness. These world-rulers keep the world overshadowed by sin, and thus they keep multitudes, whether wholly or partially, from him who is "The Light of the world." The devil and his kingdom are full of darkness (Rev. 16:10). As we think of the millions in heathen darkness, and of further millions in civilized lands still under "the power of darkness" (Col. 1:13), how we should earnestly pray that they might be brought out of their darkness into God's marvelous light. Because it is the scene of sin, the earth is dark, with the shadows of delusion, woe, and death over it. Gross darkness, fostered by its evil potentates, covers the people, and we should be

conscious of their activity, and wrestle against them as
they strive to prevent us living as "children of light, and
. . . of the day" (1 Thess. 5:5).

5. The Spiritual Forces of Evil in the Heavenly Sphere (Eph. 6:12)

The "spiritual wickedness" of the ASV is given in the
margin as "wicked spirits." Weymouth's version is somewhat similar to Moffatt's: "the spiritual hosts of evil arrayed
against us in the heavenly warfare." As "the prince of the
power of the air," Satan has his hosts operating in the
region above the earth. They are thus distinguished from
material beings and forces. Their sphere of action is
invisible and boundless. We do not realize, as we should,
that when we pray, we have to prevail over these fearful
ranks of evil and darkness ever alert to intercept our
communications with heaven.

There are those who seem to teach that we should think
more of our own heavenly experience and warfare here
below than of the sphere where wicked spirits dwell. But,
surely, there is no stage in the life of a believer when he is
so exposed to the subtle and dangerous assault of Satan as
when he is consciously seated in the heavenlies with
Christ. To be left unmolested by Satan is no evidence of
blessing. Perhaps he knows that those whose spiritual
aspirations are very low are not worth troubling about. If
we are a trouble to him, we can rest assured that he will
trouble us. Daring to rebuke the works of darkness, we can
expect the onslaught of the spiritual forces of evil. When
old forms of sin are conquered, the enemy will devise
more subtle forms, spiritual in character, directed against
our spiritual disaster.

Ever bent on corrupting us from the simplicity that is in
Christ, Satan strives to gain the advantage over us. It is,
therefore, imperative not to be ignorant of his devices (2
Cor. 2:11; 11:3). As Barnes reminds us in his *Notes:*

Satan does not approach us in repulsive forms, but comes to recommend some plausible doctrine, to lay before us some temptation that shall not immediately repel us. He presents the World in an alluring aspect; invites us to pleasures that seem harmless; and leads us in indulgence, until we have gone so far that we cannot retreat.

Our only hope of meeting his insidious attacks victoriously is on resurrection ground. Jesus arose from the grave a mighty Victor o'er his foes, and, by grace, we can share in his triumph when in combat with the same satanic foes.

The Armor

Soldiers of any national army are never asked to provide their uniform, accoutrements, and weapons for service and warfare. Once they enlist, all that is required is freely and fully provided. It is so with those who enlist in the army of the heavenly King. Their armor is what he supplies: "The armour of *God*." It must be taken, or received, and then "put on," or worn. Actually, the complete armor is Christ himself in all his fulness. "Put on as your armour the Lord Jesus Christ, and make no provision for the passions of your lower nature" (Rom. 13:14, Weymouth).

To don "the armour of light," is the equivalent of the appropriation of all Christ is in himself, and of all he has provided for us. Thus the various parts of the armor he has for his soldiers typify the attributes he possesses, and which become ours by faith, namely, *truth, righteousness, peace, faith, salvation, the Word, spirit of intercession*. It is by these virtues that we are able to resist the devil when we confront him in the day of testing, and emerge from the contest wearing the laurel of victory.

Paul uses the military metaphor of "soldiers" to describe the warfare of the saints with evil forces. The Lord chose us to be his soldiers, and if we would be "good" ones, we must be prepared to "endure hardness." Weymouth's

version is helpful at this point: "As a good soldier of Christ
Jesus accept your share of suffering. Every one who serves
as a soldier avoids becoming entangled in the affairs of civil
life, so that he may satisfy the officer who enlisted him" (2
Tim. 2:3,4). Shakespeare in *Macbeth* has the line, "God's
soldier be he," and every true believer is God's soldier.
Tennyson calls upon us to lend an ear to Plato where he
says:

> That men like soldiers may not quit the post
> Allotted by the gods.

As God has allotted to us to be his soldiers we must not
quit our post, but remain at it until called to higher
services. Let me quote Shakespeare again. He makes
Octavius say, "He's a tried and valiant soldier." This is
what each of us must be. Robert Browning could write of:

> The soldier-saints, who row on row,
> Burn upward each to his point of bliss.

As God's "soldier-saints," we must unitedly, burn upward
to our point of bliss, namely, the divine Captain himself
who is prominent in the armor Paul enumerates. If we
"strengthen [ourselves] in the Lord and in the power
which His supreme might imparts" (Eph. 6:10,
Weymouth), then we are invincible. This is the truth
Charles Wesley mentions in his militant hymn:

> Soldiers of Christ, arise,
> And put your armour on,
> Strong in the strength which God supplies
> Through His eternal Son;
> Strong in the Lord of Hosts,
> And in His mighty power,
> Who in the strength of Jesus trusts
> Is more than conqueror.

Four times over in the narrative Paul uses the term *stand* (Eph. 6:11,13,14). "Withstand" implies "stand your ground," and implies the same stationary position enabling us to resist all the attacks of our satanic foe. We are to stand our ground clothed in our armor, and fight to the end, if we would remain victors on the field. Brave and fearless, we must be "stedfast and unmovable" until the end. "To stand" conveys the idea of a calm, well-balanced stedfastness and unflinching courage, such as Mary displayed when she *stood* by the cross on which her Son and Savior was dying. John Bunyan named one of his characters *Mr. Standfast*, who, because he never yielded ground to evil or error, when "he passed over, the trumpets sounded for him on the other side." We are all familiar with the story of the soldier they found after the dreadful eruption of Mount Vesuvius, Pompeii, in 79 A.D. Although dead, he was crystallized standing at his post. Against unnumbered foes, we must stand up for Jesus "till every foe is vanquished, And Christ is Lord indeed."

The "evil day" is the day of battle, the dark crisis of the campaign against the devil and his evil hosts, and our only way of dislodging and defeating them, our only possible vantage ground of victory is union and communion with our living and ever-conquering Lord. The warrior-saints John describes overcame their satanic accuser and adversary by the blood of the Lamb.

> Stand then in His great might,
> With all His strength endued.

Our responsibility is to be sure of our standing in Christ Jesus. Paul, referring to the temptations of the devil common to men, has the solemn warning, "Let the man who thinks he stands secure beware of falling " (1 Cor. 10:12). Like Daniel may we be found standing, divinely supported, in our lot at the end of the day (12:13). "Having done all, to stand." May grace be ours to stand in his strength alone!

We now come to the order of the pieces of armor Paul gives us in his magnificent passage of contest and conquest. The apostle's close and long contact with Roman guards gave him the most effective metaphors of Christian conflict. The Christian life is a battle against satanic foes, and to make us victorious, efficient, and invincible, armor has been provided. Having often watched his guards dress for duty or battle, Paul enumerates the order in which they donned their armor. Belt and corselet met together and formed the body-armor, the greaves and the breastplate. Then came the sandals or shoes—then the helmet, and finally the taking up of his sword. Thus, the Epistle closes with the magnificent and elaborate description of the full panoply of God for his soldiers.

Our foes are of a formidable nature but God has provided armor and weapons adapted to spiritual warfare and able to protect us as we maintain a vigorous and ceaseless battle:

The truth of God is our *belt* to keep the armor in place.

The righteousness of God is our *breastplate*—the breastplate of faith and love—which protects the heart, the center of our physical life (Isa. 11:5; 59:17; 1 Thess. 5:8).

The gospel of peace forms our *sandals* or shoes and makes possible swiftness of foot, which is of great consequence in military movements.

The faith in which we stand is our *shield* whereby we are able to quench all the fiery darts of the devil. Sometimes darts set ablaze, and set fire to the enemy's clothing, camp, or house. American Indians used to fling poisoned arrows. Who can stand against the arrows of the Almighty (Job 6:4)? Against the arrows of our adversary, God himself is our Shield (Ps. 84:11).

The perfect salvation is our *helmet* and is sufficient to

protect our head with all its powers of thought and
action (Prov. 10:6).
The whole Word of God is our sword, the unfailing
offensive and effective weapon with which to defeat the
enemy (Matt. 4:1–11; Heb. 4:12).

Because of the necessity of mobility of movement no
mention is made of armor for the knees. The Christian
soldier, however, has mighty, prevailing prayer as the
invincible covering for his knees as they are bowed before
God (Eph. 3:14; 6:18). If it is true that an "army moves on
its stomach," is it not truer to say that Christ's army, the
Church Militant, fights her way to victory on its knees?
And because "more things are wrought by prayer than this
world dreams of," may we be found among God's mighty
intercessors. We pray fighting, and fight praying. The
gracious Intercessor himself within us nerves us for conflict
and inspires us to pray, always pray, for the Holy Spirit
knows that—

> He stands best who kneels most.
> He stands strongest who kneels weakest.
> He stands longest who kneels lowest.

Stirred, then, by the Spirit may we be found among the
warriors who, because of unceasing prayer, cause Satan
and his hosts to tremble and flee. Unfailing prayer is the
mightiest weapon of all against all satanic assaults.

Stand praying { Always / With all Prayer / In the Spirit / And watching } for all Saints

It will be observed that no armor is provided for the
back of the soldier for he is in the army to face the foe, not
run away from him. If he does, he can expect an arrow in
his unprotected back. Our _back_ is well protected for the
Lord besieges us _behind_ as well as _before_, and encamps

round about us (Pss. 34:8,9; 139:5). As "good soldiers of Jesus Christ" we must not shrink from the intense warfare, separation from a devil-controlled world, and obedience to a spiritually enlightened conscience it entails. The more pronounced our spiritual witness is, the greater the satanic antagonism. But fully armed, we are more than conquerors over the evil forces arrayed against us. When we take, and put on, all the armor God has provided, then we can fight the good fight of faith with strength and majesty and confidence of victory.

It is of no use having suitable armor, if we never wear it. We must be fully armed, for Satan is adept at finding the weakest spot in our defense. Of Achilles, the hero of mythology, the story is told how his mother dipped him, when a baby, in the river Lethe to make him invulnerable. His whole body was immersed except the heel by which she held him. This one omission proved fatal for an enemy discovered this unguarded spot, and shot at the heel, and killed the hero. Charles Wesley has taught us to sing—

> Leave no unguarded place,
> No weakness of the soul
> Take every virtue, every grace,
> And fortify the whole:
> To keep your armour bright,
> Attend with constant care,
> Still walking in your Captain's sight,
> And watching unto prayer.

Satan, because of the old nature in us, works in us and fights in us, but he cannot reign. He may annoy, but he cannot destroy. His authority has been destroyed by Christ, and his power is weakened by grace. He is warned to leave his old residence, and before long he will be ejected from the world. The saints have to fight, not only with Satan and the world, but with the deep and direful depravity within them, and with unbelief and carnal reason. True faith has to fight for victory, for a crown, and for God's glory and does so in God's strength—with a certainty arising from his faithful promises which are intended to encourage us in the contest. Looking to Him who is the Captain of our salvation, animates us for the combat and assures our hearts of conquest. A verse from Sherwin's militant hymn reads—

> Strong to meet the foe,
> Marching on we go,
> While our cause we know
>   Must prevail;
> Shield and banner bright
> Gleaming in the light,
> Battling for the right,
>   We ne'er can fail.

This is the spirit in which we can and must face our adversary, the devil!